The Unyielding Passion for Life of Lee Raymond Blanchette, a Remarkable Man

Kathleen Ingfried Haskins

outskirts
press

The Unyielding Passion for Life of Lee Raymond Blanchette, a Remarkable Man
All Rights Reserved.
Copyright © 2021 Kathleen Ingfried Haskins
v4.0 r1.2

The opinions expressed in this manuscript are solely the opinions of the author and do not represent the opinions or thoughts of the publisher. The author has represented and warranted full ownership and/or legal right to publish all the materials in this book.

This book may not be reproduced, transmitted, or stored in whole or in part by any means, including graphic, electronic, or mechanical without the express written consent of the publisher except in the case of brief quotations embodied in critical articles and reviews.

Outskirts Press, Inc.
http://www.outskirtspress.com

ISBN: 978-1-9772-3487-2

Cover Photo © 2021 Kathleen Ingfried Haskins. All rights reserved - used with permission.

Outskirts Press and the "OP" logo are trademarks belonging to Outskirts Press, Inc.

PRINTED IN THE UNITED STATES OF AMERICA

Disclaimer

Most dialogue and quotes are approximate, as they are from old memory. However the last chapter is verbatim, exactly as it happened. It burned into my soul, and I wrote it down before I could forget the exactness.

*FOR LEE
FROM WHOM I LEARNED
HOW TO GIVE FREELY
AND WHAT IT MEANS
TO LOVE WITH PASSION*

My gratitude goes out with thanks and Blessings to the following people for their powerful critique and wise suggestions:

My sister, Jacqueline Haskins, who is an up and coming writer

The Reverend Marguerite Unwin Voelkel, whose passions are her granddaughter, and Celtic Spirituality, and whose ministry was "to the least, the last, and the lost" before retirement

Sally Wingert, who is a vibrant actress par excellance of long standing

My Pastor, Jane McBride, who gives incredible, pertinent, timely, often memorable, even life changing, sermons

Jean Chagnon, who is a no nonsense, force to be reckoned with, does exacting analysis and grant writing, and is passionate about environmental and social justice.

And to the following two books for their creative ideas:

"Tell It Slant: Creating, Refining, and Publishing Creative Nonfiction, Third Edition" by Brenda Miller and Suzanne Paola

"Writing Down the Bones: Freeing the Writer Within" 30th anniversary edition by Natalie Goldberg

TABLE OF CONTENTS

Foreword i
Passion 1
Wild Young One 3
A Chip on His Shoulder 15
Table Talk 22
Illness 26
Mellowing Out 28
Love 34
Friends and Enemies 40
Can Do! 55
Boat Your Vote 58
Too Comfortable 60
Mission Lodge 64
River Run 76
Mom 80
Homeless 83
Redemption 90

Siamese Fighting Fish 101
Songs He Wrote 106
Falling Off the Wagon 109
Justin and Sky 112
Sick Again 116
Santa Claus 121
ICOM 123
How Could It Be?! 125
Afterword 135

FOREWORD
by Denny, Lee's mentor

Hi Kathy,

Your book came yesterday and I finished it today. I can't believe how well it was done. As I was reading, many of the missing pieces of Lee's life came into focus. While we may have talked frequently, he almost never told me in an honest and complete way what was going on in his life from his Plymouth time, living in his van, the apartments he rented, and the succumbing to prescribed painkillers. He kept most everything all bottled up, pretending everything was OK and he was doing well.

You did a wonderfully true and honest description of Lee's talents and foibles. In spite of his shortcomings, there was a spirit and passion in his life and in everything he did. He could make me, and you, so angry so as to not want to have anything to do with him and still, when he got it together, still want to share in his achievements and accomplishments. It was hard to stay mad at Lee.

During our low points, my wish was that he could overcome the pull of the bottle. He had everything so many would give anything to possess to be successful, admired, respected, and appreciated. We could see that side of Lee shining out during his times of sobriety. With his talents, he did not need to live a life of poverty.

Please earmark the enclosed check towards putting your book in the hands of a few of his friends that perhaps can't afford it or in places where it will be passed around for others to see. Those that knew Lee well should understand the nature and stature of the man that walked in their midst.

Thank you for writing the book. The love and caring you shared is a tribute to both him and you. Few in life have a friend like you.

As Lee would often say, "Mission Accomplished."

Denny

PASSION

"The human body is a miraculous machine; however it is the soul and passion for life that forever endures. Being faced with a variety of both physical and psychological adversity, I've found through the years an unyielding passion for life and a desire to become empathetic towards others. My experience is one of many that with compassion, the ability to serve, strive, and not to yield, may one day serve the principle purpose that those with similar misfortune and experiences may continue to learn and grow. My name is Lee Raymond Blanchette, this is my story…

"Here, Kathy! How do you like the outline for my book?"
"That's not an outline, Lee; that is an introductory paragraph."
"It is my outline. I will expand on it."

When Lee first rented a room in my house, he had two immediate goals. The first was to paddle down the whole length of the Mississippi River from its birth waters to the ocean in New Orleans, in his kayak. That would make him the first above-the-knee amputee to do so. But more about his river experience later. The second was to write about the experience to encourage others to reach their potential, especially those with "handicaps." Lee would often tell me, "I do not have a handicap; it is merely an inconvenience."

WILD YOUNG ONE

Lee was a real talker. A conversation with him usually lasted an hour or more at the least. He was always telling me about his "leg," and the doctors who helped him. Then he would jump around to various things in his past. On one occasion, he was telling me about his youth. "My dad died in a car accident in Oxford when I was about three. It was a drunk driver that killed him. After my dad died, my mom hitched up with a junkie, Ron. He was just awful! I can't believe she would do that, chose a junkie over her own son!"

Lee loved the woods, the vigorous pine woods between his house and the neighboring farm of Denny and Jane. They were for him an escape from a heinous home life to the wonders of nature and freedom. Not only the freedom to drink alcohol with his friends, as Denny told me. He was at home in the woods, camping out, the lure that of being on his own where he could do whatever he wanted without interference. These woods taught him how to track deer, rabbit, ring-tailed raccoon, squirrels, and other skittish wildlife, and from their footprints he could "see" the animals in action. This knowledge proved useful later in life when he worked as a guide in the mountains.

"Denny and Jane, our neighbors, gave us a couple of goats and a couple of bee hives when Mom was with Ron, and I had a dog, Moose, who was the only good thing about that time. Ron raised Christmas trees, and they got infected by beetles. He wanted to spray for the beetles, which would kill the bees, so Denny and Jane took the bees back." (Denny said it had to be done very fast, and not at all in keeping with bee moving practices. They had to load the bee hives up in their pick-up with the hives open and all the bees flying around so the honey makers could find home, and Denny and Jane needed to wear bee keeper protective gear so as not to be stung by the mob. That not only would hurt, it would cost them even more bees, as each sting is a bee dying for the good of the hive, leaving its stinger in you, with an organ ripped from its abdomen pumping poison.) "My mom left Ron after that."

"I was also molested." (He wouldn't say by who.) "I think I survived that without lasting effect on me, but I won't go into what they did to me. So, anyway, I ran away into the woods and went to our neighbor's house. Denny and Jane's. They were very good to me. Denny would take me hiking when I was fifteen or so. That is where I first fell in love with the mountains. He took me to Vermont, and New Jersey, but I especially liked the White Mountains. Denny got to be like my surrogate dad. Then Mom took up with another guy, Danny. He pruned apple trees, and that is how they met, working in an apple orchard in Hayden Pond, him showing Mom how to prune. I was strong headed, and a handful, and didn't get on with him, either, at first. He won my respect though. I hit him over something, and he hit me back so hard that he knocked me down and broke my nose. Nobody else could ever do that." (According to Danny, Lee was beating the hood of Danny's car, putting dents in it, and refused to stop when told to.)

When Danny first started dating Lee's mother, Georgia, Danny remembers going down into the cellar for something, and Lee came down the stairs saying, "Dan, you are a nice guy; stay out of my life." Danny wanted to hit the kid, but didn't. "Eventually, Danny and I got to be good friends, and I started calling him '"Pops"' instead of '"Danny."' Pops liked that. He always did want me to think of him as his dad, and he treated me like his son, not just in no hands barred in punishments, but also, he was very supportive. He came to all my kayak races. And Pops was there in the hospital when my leg was shot up. He was there for me whatever happened. Even rented me an apartment and a garage so I could be on my own and start a business." When Lee was drunk, he could be clumsy and destructive. He and a friend borrowed Danny's fiberglass canoe once, and didn't tie it properly in the truck. The canoe fell out and got damaged. Danny made no bones about Lee needing to fix it. Lee felt bad, and made a very good patch job. But Danny was tired of living with a drunk. So he rented Lee an apartment a piece away in a six family house Danny had inherited in Southbridge—actually, let him have it for free in exchange for Lee up keeping the whole house, plumbing, electricity, carpentry, everything. Lee also was able to use its garage for free as a workshop as part of the deal. Thus, Lee's first enterprise was born—fixing and building canoes and kayaks. And he became an expert handyman.

Lee would sometimes tell me stories about his adventures in kayak racing. "I made fourth place in the Olympics! That is DAMN good. But nobody cares a fuck about the person who makes fourth. They only really care about the person who makes first place and then second and third place; but fourth place, you may as well have come in last." (Danny says it was just a regular race, not the Olympics. Probably where Lee got the idea that he was in the Olympics was from Lee's little sister, April, who won a gold medal in the Special Olympics for swimming the backstroke). "I had this thing where I would roll my kayak during the race to show the decals and expressions that I would place on the bottom. I would roll as I came into the finish line where the most observers were, then come back up again. And Pops saw it all!" Actually, Danny chose to watch at the dangerous rapids, and never saw Lee turn over. He says Lee's interest in canoes, kayaks, and racing all started with him letting Lee use his canoe, dropping Lee in the river at one point, and picking him up again a couple of hours later farther downstream. To say that Lee loved the water is an understatement.

Lee proved a handful for everybody, including his teachers. "I never graduated high school." He was always honest about it and regretful. On more than one occasion while he lived with me he tried to get his GED. "School was too boring, and I wanted to be active, outside in the woods." (His dad, Danny, says he was extremely wild, and probably got moved forward a grade each year out of the teacher's desire not to have him again. His mentor, Denny, says that whenever he wanted something in school, he would get his way by going berserk; Lee was unruly, and could be ruthless. Denny told me that when Lee was sixteen and they had come out of the White Mountains, Denny paid some guy to take him to the other trail head to pick up his car, while Lee waited for him. When Denny got back, Lee had some kid cowering because he had questioned Lee's ability to climb the mountain.

Once Danny married Georgia, and the family moved to Woodstock, Connecticut, Denny did not see as much of Lee. Denny did, however, help Lee out by letting him do some work. Lee put siding on Denny's house when Lee was twenty eight. But then, Lee didn't want to use the safety measures, and also continued to drink. Denny decided he could not have Lee assist him any longer, as it was dangerous work anyway, and Lee was just compounding the danger and liability. Again, they did not have much contact until 1996 when Lee came to borrow money from Denny. Lee was thirty years old at the time, and wanted $1000.00 to buy a car. Denny says Lee brought a very unsavory character with him, which Denny did not appreciate, as he had a lot of valuable equipment stored in his barns. But he did loan Lee the money, interest free for a year, on the condition that Lee repay him in installments; otherwise Denny would charge him interest. Lee never repaid the debt, and he stopped calling Denny for a long time after that.

Another time in the first year Lee rented from me, he told me, "Growing up, I've always been fascinated by early explorers breaking new ground, setting standards that years later have followed me into my adult life. Jacques Yves Cousteau, Edward Shackleton, Perry and North, to name a few, were some of my early heroes from the ages of seven to thirteen." Lee was fascinated by Jacques Cousteau and his life on the water studying and filming fish, coral, sting rays, sharks, and all other ocean life. He wanted fish of his own to watch.

"I had fish when I was a teen," he continued. "It started with a goldfish, and then I got a tank, and then I had several tanks. They lined the room. That's a lot of work, draining, cleaning, and refilling so many tanks. But I loved it. I knew the name of every type of fish. Maybe I'll get an aquarium again." Danny doesn't know what happened to all the fish and tanks. They did not accompany Lee when Georgia married Danny and she and her family moved in with him.

And his fascination with Shackleton, Perry and North, led Lee to want to go to the Antarctic to live, to work, to be. It was on his Bucket List. A lifelong desire of his, for which he was continually trying to make adjustments to his "leg" so that it would function in that kind of cold. Lee liked the cold, thrived in winter, just that his "leg" would freeze up on him when it got cold; the fluid inside wasn't rated for the cold temperatures even of Minnesota. He was very inventive. A couple important improvements he made to the design of his prosthetic leg were: getting a pivoting ankle (he got the idea from ball bearings), and coming up with a heated unit to go around the socket his stump fit into so he could do his snow removal and not be cold.

Lee's Bucket List also consisted of swimming with the dolphin named Winter. Poor Winter had entangled her tail in the rope of a blue crab trap when she was three months old in August 2011. The rope cut off blood circulation to her tail. She lost her tail, but a devoted young boy, an excellent prosthetics doctor, and a marine biologist, came to the rescue. They outfitted her with a prosthetic tail that had a gel liner, and rehabilitated her enough to survive and return to health. This was done at the Clearwater Marine Hospital, and she is now at the Clearwater Marine Aquarium in Florida. The technology used was considered a "ground breaking miracle," which not only saved Winter, but could save "countless people everywhere in the world." A whole movie was made about Winter, called "Dolphin Tale," and she "remains a symbol of hope, courage and perseverance to all the millions of people who learn of her, disabled and able bodied persons alike."

Lee really identified with Winter, both because she had a prosthesis like he had, and because he considered himself a dolphin. He wanted to swim with his alter-ego and make connection. Actually, Lee identified with all animals and people with limb loss. He subscribed to the "inMotion" magazine for people "with limb loss and limb difference," and kept trying to get me to read it, too. The only person with limb loss that Lee did not identify with was Aron Ralston. Ralston had cut off his own arm at the elbow to save his life when a big bolder fell and pinned him in a desolate part of a desert, and nobody knew of his where-a-bouts in order to look for him. Lee thought Ralston exploited his story for monetary gain, and Lee thought that was wrong. Lee wanted to paddle the Mississippi River and write about it, not for money but to encourage other persons with short-comings or "handicaps" to dream big, and to live their dreams.

He showed me his dolphins; a pair, swimming intertwined, diving, tattooed over his ribs on his right side. He was very proud of them, and of himself. "I am a dolphin," he told me. "Dolphins rescue people. I've done a lot of recovery work in my days. When I had my dog, Molly, we were a team." And then he described dead bodies found under water, how to tell how long they had been there, what to place under your nose so the smell of rotting flesh didn't overwhelm you. It was interesting, but gross, so I won't repeat any of it. And then, on the calf of his natural leg, he showed me his tattoo, this one in colors of green and red, of a canoeist going over a waterfall, again, to represent himself. In his younger years, he succeeded in doing that a couple of times, and got picked up by the police for it because it was so crazy dangerous. But Lee was proud of it.

Lee had a tender side to him that made him lovable. He had been in Outward Bound **twice**, once at Hurricane Island, and once at Voyageur. Outward Bound's motto of "to strive to serve and not to yield" was the philosophy of life by which Lee lived every moment of every day. He was constantly reminding me that **that** was the proper way to live one's life.

"My first experience of adventure wasn't the building and construction of a clubhouse," he told me, "but one of an Outward Bound poster I saw when I was at a doctor's appointment with my mother. I believe I was 8 or 9 years old. It was on the second floor of the Family Primary Doctors office, and it looked too cool to my youthful eyes, being at the highest point and relying on nothing but you own laurels and teamwork."

Starting December 26, 1984, when Lee was 17, he went camping for ten days in the middle of winter, in frigid temperatures in the Mahoosuc Mountains with Outward Bound. It was a program for troubled youth—no smoking, no drinking, and, of course, no television. The local paper interviewed him about the experience. Although he didn't like the carbohydrate diet (Lee is very much a meat eater), lost about ten pounds, and missed playing his guitar, he loved the snow, hiking and snowshoeing, and just being in the mountains, and wanted to do it all again. Lee's mom was also interviewed in the article, and the article quotes her as saying, [Outward Bound programs] "build self confidence. Meeting the challenge and learning the skills of survival is a great experience for kids....The program gets young people working together as a group...the comradeship is especially strong. They rely on others as they never did before and yet learn to be independent. They appreciate dry feet and warm sleeping bags." One thing that did not get put into the article, but that he told me about, was that one day he realized one of the girls had fallen behind everyone else, so he went back to look for her. She was shivering, hypothermic. Lee put her into his sleeping bag and got in with her, not to have sex, he admonished me, but to warm her up, because she was so cold.

Lee was proud of what he had learned with Outward Bound, and decided he wanted a Vets T-shirt from Outward Bound. This is the letter he got back from an instructor at Voyageur:

> Lee,
> It was truly a pleasure meeting you. Hearing you speak about your Outward Bound experience and how it played a huge role in your life was heart-warming. I feel validated in the work I do because of people like you, people who tell their story. Who have dealt with adversity and come out of it stronger. More mentally tough.
>
> I respect you Lee. Within the first few minutes of meeting and then speaking to you, it was there. Because of what you've done, and how you choose to continue living your life.

Choosing not to take your Pin of Excellence at Graduation is a very difficult thing to do. It takes humility, honesty, self-awareness, and courage.

We have a saying here, which I love, and I think it is applicable here: "Outward Bound can only ignite. It is up to you to keep the flame alive." I'm glad to see you've held up your end of the bargain, Lee.

Congratulations.

P.S. We don't have any more Vets T-shirts. But I was able to find this patch. Wear both your Pin and Patch with Pride.

"So, I bet you're wondering how I lost my leg." He said to me one day, bemused that I hadn't asked him yet. "I could tell you I lost it in the military, or in a climbing accident, and you wouldn't know different. The truth is neither. Are you interested?"

"Yes, I am interested; I just didn't think it was any of my business."

"The truth is, I got shot in the leg. I was answering an EMS call, only I had been drinking. I didn't think I would be called anymore that day. It was a domestic dispute, and I got angry, and the husband came at me with a gun and shot me right in the leg, not once, but twice! It was gushing blood, and I had to tear off my shirt to tie around my leg for a tourniquet. I was in shock, and had to drive to the hospital myself that way, using my left leg to work the gas and the brakes."

His dad tells me that according to the husband, it was self defense; Lee left, then came back after him with a two by four. When Lee was confronted by the police in his hospital room to get his side of the story, Lee would only yell at them "Contact my lawyer!" although he didn't have a lawyer. According to Lee's mentor, Denny, shootings are always investigated. One of Lee's uncles was a state trooper, and the story that he obtained was that Lee had done some carpentry work building a porch for this man, a person of importance in the area, and Lee was coming around to collect money before the job was over—and Lee was drunk. In self defense, the man shot him in the front yard.

"The wound went clear down to the bone, and every day when the nurses cleaned it out it hurt like hell so bad I would scream bloody murder, and it would take four of them just to hold me down, while someone else swabbed it out. Finally, I yelled at them to cut it off; that if they didn't, I would. And I took a marker and made a dotted line where I wanted it cut. At first it was a below-the-knee amputation, but then I went on a climbing wall without a bilinear and fell twenty feet. I landed on my feet and hands, and the fall jammed my bones; it broke bones in my arms and wrists, which have metal plates in them now, my left ankle broke, and my right leg had to go through surgery again. I've been through so many surgeries and radiation treatments to stop the bone from growing spurs, and each time, my leg gets shorter. Last time, they took a slab of skin off my back to cap off my stump." And he lifted his shirt so I could see his left shoulder blade, scarred and indented from the removal. (According to Lee on a later account, there was about a year and a half between the shooting and when the amputation was done. This was corroborated by his mentor, Denny, who said he still had his leg, although it was very fragile, when he climbed Bancroft Tower, drunk, without safety gear, to impress some lady. Bancroft Tower is about thirty or forty feet high; Lee never made it to the top, and lost his leg from his fall from the tower, around the year 1990 when he would have been twenty four.)

A CHIP ON HIS SHOULDER

When Lee answered my ad of looking for a housemate, I was a little unsure of him. He brought a resume, and brought a friend with him, who vouched that Lee was a nice guy, only their household could no longer keep him. Both of them were pretty quiet during the interview, seeming to think that the resume said everything I needed to know, although it did not spell out past living situations, nor explain how he would pay rent. It did say that Lee had his own business, "Paddlers Plus— Just add water: Limitations, Challenge, Change." Lee wanted me to look it up on the internet, which I did, but the web page was mostly a picture of two dolphins swimming together. Nothing about what the business did. I had two fully furnished rooms available at the time. One had an alcove in the hall way. The other, that Lee liked, had a private "tree house" deck, with a large Box Elder shading the whole of it, keeping it cool in the summer. The main branch passed close to the rail so that the leafy twigs hid you from view below. Such privacy! And yet an excellent lookout to keep watch over the neighborhood. Yes, to dwell with nature, not need to purchase furniture, and observe goings-on with stealth. Lee found it perfect for him. We sat in this room for the interview.

"One thing I want to tell you," I said, "Is that I have schizoaffective disorder. It is kinda like a cross between manic depression and schizophrenia. I am on meds for it, have pledged to myself to stay on meds, and have been stable for 18 years now. I can give you references of what I am like to live with. Basically, I am like anybody else, now that I am on meds, but I want to make sure that no housemate of mine is going to get weirded-out over it after moving in, and that is why I am telling you now."

"I used to have a fiancé that was manic depressive," he answered, "So I know how it goes, and I am not afraid of it."

He seemed to be able to maneuver the flight of stairs alright, even with his "inconvenience." His eagerness was infectious. Something told me that this was really important; Lee needed the room badly, wanted it even more. Whatever the troubles, I was betting that in the long run, it would be good to have him here. So he moved in June 1st, 2011.

A carpenter by trade, Lee was constantly looking around my house for things he could do for money. He noticed some wood stripping pulling away from my island countertop, in front of my kitchen sink, and above the sink near the window. He drew up a proposal for me, and wrote out a release of responsibility form that read:

July 1, 2011
From: Lee Raymond Blanchette.
Owner) of Said Property: 2108 Millwalke Ave (really Milwaukee)
        Minneapolis, MN 55406 (really 55404)
Mr Mrs. Loren and Patti Haskins.
Agent) Mrs. Kathy Haskins Residing at Same. (In reality, I have never been married, but my correcting him always frustrated him)
Waive all Rights Under Minnesota State law
Per Renters Agreement
I.E. this is Also to Include Release:
  * of Any Slip and Fall
  *use of Power Equipment
  *Entrance & Egress
  *Medical Coverage & Insurance
Owner) of Said Property Mr Mrs Loren and Patti Haskins (and then gave my parents address and phone, Lee's signature, and the date again.)

Reading it is ambiguous. Is it Lee who is waiving rights, or the Haskins'? Lee wanted to make sure that we would hire him, so he drew this up very seriously to waive HIS rights, to release US of fault. Oh well. It is now just a memory, him declaring no one would hire him because he was a liability with his leg. At any rate, I decided to hire him and see what he could do. He attached the wood strips alright, but it was a very unsightly job. He had glued and screwed the strips into place, and left the screws visible! He was proud of his work, and eager to show off to me how tight the seams were now, but I was ready to cry. "No, Lee! How could you?! Those strips looked better before! They were pure wood! You couldn't tell how they were attached!"

Lee was crestfallen. "I'll fix it. I'll recess the screws, and fill in with wood fill."

It helped. But I looked at those blond circles on the golden wood grain, and decided then and there I would have to be more careful what I let Lee do.

The legaleze went the other way, too. Lee needed to balance on one leg to take a shower, the other leg just being a stump with the prosthesis off. The rough surface of my tub floor had been worn fairly smooth, so Lee wanted a bath mat to stand on. Very reasonable, and fairly cheap to get. But Lee wanted to make sure I got it right away, so he threatened to sue me if I didn't go get one the day he moved in. He showed me the calling card for his lawyer. Really? You've got to threaten me over something like that? It left a bitter taste in my mouth.

It didn't take long to figure out why the other household could not keep Lee any more. The friend had said something about no more room, time limits for occupants and such, but I think there were other, even more important reasons. Lee had a chip on his shoulder as big as a house, and used lots of foul language. One of his favorite phrases was, "FUCK YOU AND DIE!!!" He had a saying that I wish I could remember in full because it was so poetic: "I'm your WORST FUCKIN' NIGHTMARE, over a DARK MOON RISING…" and then it went on a couple more spooky stanzas. He also made a habit of borrowing money, a little here and a little there, until it amounted to quite a bit—sometimes over $100. I always kept track of how much he owed me because he was constantly asking for a few bucks. He several times suggested I should be the accountant for his business because I kept such close attention to detail. It turned out that he was on social security disability, and that is how he paid rent. On the first of the month, he paid rent, paid off all his debts, and then started borrowing again, sometimes even the same day. He was a smoker, which I did not like, but had agreed to during the interview as long as he only smoked outside. But the worst of all was that he was an alcoholic.

Lee's favorite alcohol was whiskey. He at times drank beer, but he was really a Jack Daniel's whiskey man. He would drink straight from the bottle, and savor it. He loved to go sit on a weathered, wooden picnic table in Matthew's Park under deciduous trees where a path passed the grassy, tree covered hill. The hill was free of trees on the other side, steep and used for sledding in the winter. He called this spot "his office." He would drink until he could barely walk, and then would come home, if still capable. I have memories of going to the park and seeking him out to see if he needed help. Sometimes he would be picked up by police or an ambulance and taken to de-tox. I remember waiting with him in the park late at night one time until the ambulance arrived. He did drink in his room as well. I got into locking my bedroom door at night, because I didn't trust him, and he could be violent when drinking. I was glad, too, about my decision because one night when he had too much to drink, he came pounding on my door, yelling at me, then tried to open the door. When it didn't yield to him, he went away, yelling his favorite phrase. Needless to say, I did not sleep well that night.

Another day, Lee was being so problematic that I called the police. I don't remember the situation exactly; all I remember is that it took *four, big* police officers to wrangle him up off the floor where he threw himself to keep from being taken. It took *all four* of them to muscle him down the stairs, and out to the waiting vehicle to take him away. I was so amazed at his strength, that it surpassed my fear.

Lee was something else when he was drunk. The significant other of a friend of mine says when Lee became drunk in a bar, he would try to take on all the customers at once! He got 86ed (kicked out for good) from Palmer's, which really made Lee sad on account they had a group of musicians called the "Hootenannies." The Hootenannies would gather there to play blue grass and old time music, and they used to let Lee play with them.

He also got 86ed out of Hard Times Café, very disappointing to him because Hard Times was the favorite hangout of Lee's best friend and side-kick Joe. Hard Times had a Free Box, and Joe on occasion would try to bring me something from it. I usually declined his presents, but he did bring me some turquoise once that I asked a friend to make into a necklace for me.

Lee's ability to fight served him well when he was sober. There was a time he went to the corner Holiday gas station to buy cigarettes, candy, and Poweraid. There he witnessed a gang of seven youth attack an older Black gentleman as he was putting gas into his car. The man hid under his car to escape the onslaught, no one coming to his aid. Up walks Lee, and the group thought they had it made, thought they had an easy victim what with his prosthetic. Lee took on those seven chaps who surrounded him in attack.

I can visualize Lee's skill, now a right punch, now a left, pivoting on his prosthetic, knocking each assailant to the ground. Another quick spin, knocking down the next person before the others could get up. Blow after powerful blow, taking down the enemy; slams and punches to the head and gut that a boxer would be proud of, could brag about, until the gang finally fled. Yes, he could really fight.

TABLE TALK

Nights after I came home from work, we would sit at the dining room table, or stand in the back yard so he could smoke, and talk of all kinds of subjects.

"So, I bet you're wondering how I got to Minnesota from Connecticut. I wasn't about to spend my life in a crappy little town! I got a job with Wilderness Inquiry, and that meant Minnesota. I was looking forward to teaching kayaking and canoeing, but instead, they wanted me to give pep talks to disabled persons, especially returning vets. I didn't want to be a poster boy for them, so I quit. But here I was in Minneapolis, so I made it home, though I miss the mountains. How about you, have you lived here all your life?"

"No, I was born in Denver, Colorado. I miss the mountains, too. We used to spend a lot of time in the mountains, skiing in the winter and hiking the rest of the year. How I got here was following my family. My dad went back to school to get a PhD in Math. Then we began the process of searching the whole country for where he could become a professor. We visited a couple of colleges as a family, and then Dad visited Carleton on his own. Mom and Dad asked us kids where we thought we ought to live, and Dad work. It was obvious that the best situation for Dad would be at Carleton, and we liked the idea of the Arboretum. It seemed inevitable to me, so I voted we go there. I wanted my parents to feel good about the decision, besides I had lost touch with my friends. I don't know what my sister's reasoning was. Much later, my parents told me that we would have stayed in Denver if that is what we kids voted for. That shows true parental love. They always treated us with respect, and as adults. Anyway, the summer of my thirteenth year, we moved to Northfield."

"You've got great parents."

"Speaking of parents, I want your emergency contact information, in case anything should ever happen."

"O.K. I'll leave it with you as long as you don't contact my parents. Don't contact them unless I am like, dying. Otherwise, contact Joe."

"As you wish. But I would like your parents address and phone. Your date of birth would be good, too."

He gave me the information. "Hey, John Lennon was shot on your birthday! I only know that because I have a friend who is really into John Lennon, and says he was shot the day before my birthday. My birthday falls on the day of ascension of Mary. I can't compete with Mary in holiness, but I do try to respect my being born on that day by being a worthwhile person."

Lee continually introduced me to his friends. He wanted me to know him inside out, his friends as well. This included his Pastor, and the church he belonged to, where he lived before he rented from me. They put on a dinner for me, at the house where they all lived together. The big table did not fit everyone, but spirits were high; lots of joking. The place was a mess, with the back door open, and live chickens wandering through the house. An "experience" for sure. I realized Lee was not as unwanted here as I had imagined. Lee had very close relationships with some of the members of the church house. It through new light on what he was like, and I felt guilty and embarrassed for my previous bad thoughts.

One day I came home from work and Lee was lying in the driveway where the stairs go up to the porch. I had to pull in carefully so as not to run over his head, which disappeared from view as I pulled in. "Must be another drunken episode," I thought, and called 911 for the ambulance to take him away. When he came back from the hospital, he told me what happened. He had just stepped out for a smoke, and on returning to the house, his prosthetic knee locked up as he was stepping up; he fell backward, hit his head, and went unconscious. Again, I felt guilty about my judging him, and scared about his falls. He fell a lot. Every time I pull into my drive now I get a squeamish feeling all over, imagining him lying there and me not being able to see him.

On another occasion, Lee came home all in a huff. "I can't believe Jim! I don't understand why he is so mad at me! I saved a dog's life!"

"What happened, Lee?"

"Right behind Welna, there was this cute little dog locked up in a car with the windows all rolled up. He was barking, and barking forlornly. I broke the window of the car and rescued him or he would have gotten heat stroke! It was so hot in the car. I took the dog to Welna where they have a bowl of water for dogs, and dog treats; boy was he thirsty! But Jim (the owner of Welna 2), was real mad at me for rescuing the dog!"

"Maybe he thought you should have tried to find the owner before breaking the window."

"Don't you get on me too! I saved the dog's fuckin' life, damn it!" For Lee, compassion and passion walked hand in hand. He saw a dog in danger, and needed to step in or he would never forgive himself.

Lee had a soft spot in his heart especially for dogs. He loved dogs of all kinds, shapes, and sizes, and invited the neighbor in a couple of times to talk, just to have the opportunity to hold the neighbor's dog on leash. Lee wanted a dog here so bad. I wouldn't let him have one. At one point I mentioned that he couldn't afford one, and his reaction was, "The dog would eat before I would." Yea, he couldn't even feed himself as it was. His friend Joe and I sometimes picked up the tab. And he wanted a dog.

ILLNESS

Lee was forever putting himself into the hospital for unbalanced potassium/chloride ratios. He would feel terrible, would guess the problem was his ratios, and he would be right. The hospital usually held him for a day or two for that. Sometimes he put himself into the hospital because his stump became raw, bruised, and peeling from working so hard on it. He needed to be hospitalized in order to get the prescription ointment to rub on the sores. For that, they just kept him a few hours, would give him the prescription, and let him go to heal at home. He didn't like being in the hospital any more than necessary.

For one, it was hard to get permission to smoke. On one occasion, he was in their smoke room with a couple of other persons, one of whom made a racist comment. Even though Lee was prejudiced against Somalis, he thought he was not racist, and he got extremely mad at this person. Having learned to control his temper some, with redirection, he punched the Plexiglas window instead of the man. Lee had a powerful punch. This

Plexiglas was the quarter inch stuff you find in banks to protect the tellers, and he cracked it he hit it so hard.

One day when it was hot and the sun was shining bright, I took Lee to Cub Foods near us to do some shopping. The transition from the bright sun light to the dimmer, flickering, fluorescent light caused Lee to have a seizure right by the greeting cards; he hit his head on a protrusion just above the left eye ball. A bump swelled to the size of a large, round marble, squirting a shot of blood six feet away. That the poke didn't get him **in** the eye is a miracle beyond miracles it came that close to grazing the eye ball. People from the store came immediately to help, had an ambulance there before you could say "1, 2, 3," and I had to warn them all not to touch the blood because he had Hepatitis C.

Lee was disgusted that he had Hepatitis C, but had gotten over the anger. He contracted it from one of the transfusions he had during one of his many surgeries. He was responsible about it, and wouldn't have a girlfriend because of it, wanted to make sure he didn't have sex and spread it to others. It put a hole in his life, though, because he wanted a girlfriend badly. He also wished he could have kids, have a family of his own. I think he saw what other people had in the way of family, and felt left out, denied something beautiful and meaningful.

MELLOWING OUT

But when sober, Lee could be very pleasant to be around, and eventually we became friends. He was truly an incredible person. He loved people, and made friends wherever he went. Whether at the register of the corner store, walking around the neighborhood, getting his hair cut, going to the doctor, or for a prosthesis adjustment, he turned business transactions into fast, lasting friendships. He had a close friendship with Jim, who owned and ran the neighborhood hardware store. His doctor gave him extra of his precious time just to sit and shoot the bull, sometimes as much as an hour, as did his prosthetic manager.

Lee was curious about everything, which sparked conversation with the people he met, and landed him employment in tree trimming, snow removal, mural painting, and, of course, carpentry. He had a way with words that made people want to do things for him. He realized his talent, and acknowledged, "I could sell a kayak to an Eskimo!" This ability increased as he dropped that chip on his shoulder, and that tendency to make everything into a legal matter. I don't think he saw it as being manipulative, but as being friendly and honest. He liked to praise people and tell them how much they meant to him. Now, who doesn't like that? For the most part, his request did not come with the praise, but was built into the conversation, or maybe didn't even come until days later after a relationship had been established. He could be very demanding and knowledgeable, and that won him respect with his orthotic/prosthetic manager, as well as with his primary care doctor, both of whom he had to see frequently and became friends with. Lee's love of people is also what brought him to doing Emergency Medical Service work, or EMS, which he did in the Outward Bound philosophy of "to strive to serve and not to yield." Doing volunteer EMS defined his life, and gave it meaning. Every day, he would make the rounds of neighborhood businesses to see if his services were needed.

Lee was always thinking of other people. He loved people, and wanted to be as helpful as possible. His tender side is what made him become an Emergency Medical Responder (EMS). I'm not sure when he started doing that on a volunteer basis, but by the time I knew him it was at the core of his Being. He kept a medical bag with him at all times. He frequently went through it on the dining room table, making sure he had all the supplies he needed, and that they were all arranged in an order that was easily accessible. When he moved in with me, he said, "Don't worry if I get up in the middle of the night and head off. As an EMS I am on call 24/7." He showed me the remote for receiving his calls.

I was forever being reminded that Lee was really and truly a very nice and friendly guy who had just been "born on the wrong side of the tracks" and therefore had a foul mouth and had to learn to fight for himself. In reality, he was down to earth, and said things as he saw them, which he called "being from the East Coast," and "having an East Coast personality." He thought Minnesotans were too soft and hid their real thoughts. But he was very friendly, making friends with all the neighbors, and persons running the neighborhood businesses. He was extremely, committedly, compassionate towards all persons and animals. He refused to eat fish, because he was a dolphin, and that would be "akin to cannibalism." And he kept his medical bag with him and at the ready at all times so he could step in on emergencies that arose in the streets.

There was this night Lee wanted to go out on the town and listen to music. He was thinking of going to a restaurant that had open mic gigs on Wednesday evenings, and asked if I wanted to come hear him play. That sounded like fun, so off we went. I had not eaten dinner yet, so while we were waiting for the time for the music to start, I ordered a sandwich. When it came, it was huge! A foot long! Too much for me, so I asked Lee if he wanted to split it. He said, "Sure." When he bit into it, he said, "Mmm! This is pretty good!" And then I remembered, "Oh, Lee! I am so sorry! I forgot. This is fish." His expression changed dramatically to one as if he had just been poisoned. He immediately jumped up, ran out the back door, and threw up in the alley. He was a dolphin through and through, and he really meant it when he said for him eating fish would be akin to cannibalism.

Lee thought "all things come in threes," bad or good. Whenever he would come to the rescue of someone, for instance, once it was a girl hit by a car and laying in the street that he treated until the paramedics could arrive, he would come home and say, "The Man Upstairs," then he would point to the sky, and continue, "He can stay in his sandbox, and I'll stay in mine." He thought of himself as being humble, but he was so *passionate* about **everything** that it would be hard to say he was humble about anything, even before God.

One day a friend of mine was visiting with one of her friends who had just fallen down and hurt her head. Lee brought out his trauma kit, and felt her head for a bump. He found none, but he played the medic to the hilt, and she was putty in his hands. "Mostly a bruised ego," was the diagnosis. We were all relieved; no concussion. While we were talking, this gal noticed a hand-sized amethyst rock I had on my knick knack shelves, and said, "Wow! Amethyst! That has great healing powers!"

"It also has the energy of Love," I added. "Would you like to have it? I have so many rocks and knick knacks that I won't miss it; besides I have another amethyst, too."

"Really?" She got all excited.

"Of course! You know the value of it, and how to use it, and that's what matters to me. It is not helping anyone here; just gathering dust."

"Thanks!"

"It makes me feel really good to give it to you." And it did. And to tell the truth, most of the time, I do not even remember it missing. But it was Lee's expertise that really made the difference.

In August, Andrew moved into the house in the middle bedroom. He was in school to be an artist. None of the three of us had cars, so Lee used the parking pad to station his kayak on top of saw horses. Lee painted a mermaid on one side of the bow, blue and green, with long, flowing auburn hair, and a similar merman on the other side of the bow with a beard and short hair. He decorated the body of the kayak with decals of Midwest Mountaineering and Winona Canoes. It was a bright red kayak, and he loved it; spent many hours painting and decorating it for days on end. He was very proud of his art work, and jumped at the chance to show it off to me. Naturally, I was appreciative. His merman held a forked magic trident like Neptune had. The finished work was quite impressive.

When he could, Lee would get someone to take him to one of the lakes to paddle around. Usually it would take the form of him giving them lessons. They'd provide the transportation; he would provide the kayak, paddles, life jackets, and rope. The lessons always worked well, with both parties feeling they got the best deal. Lee kept all his equipment in a gray, plastic "dock box" on the side of my house about waist high, four feet wide, and long enough to store paddles. Once the decorations were done on the kayak, he stored his saw horses in there, too, and kept the kayak upside-down on top.

To say Lee was strong is an understatement. He was 6'1" of pure muscle, and he'd throw his heavy kayak up onto one shoulder as if it were light as a feather, carry it to someone's car for a trip to a lake, and place it on top all by himself; (I could barely lift one end). Probably Lee's "leg" contributed to his strength; his prosthetic leg weighed over twenty pounds. Hauling that around as if it were a normal light leg made his abs tough. He also had very strong arms and hands. A handshake with him was crushing; a hug, unbearable. On one occasion, I was about to go bicycling and had my helmet on. In play, he slapped the top of my helmet; boy did it **hurt!** He teased me about how I was so weak and fragile, but the truth was it hurt as much as if I had fallen off my bicycle and hit my head! He finally did understand how strong he was, and in his last stint with me he was very careful to hug gently.

One of the things I loved about him was his guitar playing. He would practice in his room, or in the living room, put on a CD and accompany it with strumming or picking. He was not great at it, but could still do remarkably well, considering everything. A long time ago, he had been a roady, following Billy Goodspeed, playing with him, and doing the sound board. After that, he didn't have a guitar for a number of years, and was now trying to get back into it. He was very much into his music, and forever having me listen to one singer or another on his cell phone, particularly with certain songs he loved, and he was well versed. The only singers I had heard of before were Melissa Etheridge, and Janice Joplin.

Then there was silence once more in the house—he had pawned his guitar. However, he didn't stay without a guitar for long. He had his dad send him out a special, black guitar that had been his father's. This he treasured so much he had me store it for him while he later lived at Mission Lodge, and after that, sent it back east again for his nephew to play. He wanted to make sure it stayed in the family.

LOVE

"Back in my twenty's, I had this girlfriend, Trish," Lee told me. "We were very serious, but I didn't like the idea of being tied down, you know, I wanted to be able to travel, too. Six months on and six months off is **my** motto in a relationship. So one summer, I took off to Montana, and became a guide for a ranch outfit, packing hunters into the mountains, setting up their tents and gear for them, and using my knowledge of the wilds to lead them tracking down deer, or elk, or whatever they wanted to hunt. Then I would skin the animal, and cut up the meat to take back to camp, and to the ranch. You had to watch those hunters though; sometimes they wanted to do things illegal, or they would get drunk and just shoot blindly into the mountains where they could hurt someone. Once, the ranchers sent a pregnant mare on the trail with me. We didn't know how close she was to delivering because she was a big horse, and didn't show. Anyway, she delivered in camp, and the foal couldn't keep up on the return to the ranch, so I had to sling it over my horse in front of my saddle. But the day that ended it all for me was this: the hunters wanted bear; only it wasn't the season for bear, as all the little cubs were out. A cub came through camp, followed by a protective Mama bear. The hunters killed the Mama and had me skin it, left the meat, only wanted the skin and head, would have shot the cub, too, if I didn't stop them. Don't know if that cub survived. I turned in my resignation and went back to Trish—only she would not have me back. I should have stayed on the ranch in Montana. At least I would be in the mountains; I love the mountains."

"Actually, I am glad I went back to Massachusetts, because otherwise I wouldn't have met Ann," he said, wistfully. "Ann had a horse farm in Broxton with those fancy, white, high-stepping horses. She would ride them equestrian style in shows. I got a job on her horse farm because of my experience with horses. It was my job to schlep the shit, clean the stalls, put in fresh straw, curry the horses, and feed and water them. Even though I am male, the horses didn't mind being around me. That's unusual, especially for the stallions. I learned how to ride equestrian, and would exercise the horses, too. Ann and I fell in love, deeply in love, and boy did she make great sex! I might be with her today if it wasn't for my drinking. She didn't like it, particularly around the horses."

And then there was his fiancé, Sonia. The one who had manic depression. She got in trouble for stealing clothing from department stores. She would take several items into the fitting room, put them all on and walk out. She loved clothes. It was all a part of her illness.

Lee had his dog, Molly, the one that had been his partner, when he was living with his fiancé, Sonia. She was a Chocolate Lab. She was the love of his life even more than his kayak became.

She went everywhere with him. Lee accused Sonia of killing Molly because one day the dog had been with Lee, and saw Sonia on the other side of the road. When she saw her, Molly dashed across the street towards her, and a big truck mowed Molly down. Lee couldn't admit to it being an accident. In his mind, Molly shouldn't even be attached to Sonia, as Molly was Lee's dog and partner even as much as if she were a service dog. He didn't want to believe that service animals get attached to the whole family as well.

Lee left Sonia after that. He later learned that she committed suicide. He felt bad about her death, and often spoke as if he missed her, despite his accusations, hurt feelings, and her illness. He was proud of the fact that her parents liked him, too.

After Lee left Sonia, he lived for a while on a houseboat he named "The Vigilant." He kept it at the marina in Minneapolis. Something happened, though. His mentor, Denny, thinks Lee could not afford the docking fee. But that houseboat was a part of Lee, and he refused to leave her, saying, "The captain goes down with his ship!" That is when Lee's good friend, Joe, came and bodily forced him off; so Lee finally surrendered her. I guess that is when he got the idea of kayaking down the Mississippi.

One afternoon when Lee was no longer living with me, but had gone to live at Mission Lodge Sober House, he and I were seated at my dining room table chatting about romance and girlfriend/boyfriend relationships and attractions. Medicine had come far and worked wonders. While at Mission Lodge, Lee had been cured of the Hepatitis C. Now that Lee no longer had Hepatitis C, he spent a lot of time thinking about women, and how to catch a girlfriend. Then, out of the blue, he comes up with, "Now, I bet you have been at least a little attracted to me, haven't you?" He puffed himself up like a male peacock spreading its dazzling tail before a hen. I was so put off that I had to deflate him, even though, in fact I was slightly attracted to him. After all, he was physically attractive, talented, kind, thoughtful, compassionate, and had a buoyant, charming personality. However, there was no way, never, could I get it on with an alcoholic who could fall off the wagon at any time, nor with a smoker, I totally abhorred smoke, nor with a person who was so volatile.

"Nnno." I replied, succinctly and definitively, and felt some satisfaction at his disappointment. But it didn't faze him for long. Soon he was talking again about the cute UPS truck driver, and a younger woman living in the neighborhood that seemed to like him. Nothing ever could hold him down for long.

He would mention Ann again, more often, now that the Hepatitis C wasn't an impediment and he was serious about becoming sober. But he didn't want to look her up on the internet for fear that she would think he was stalking her. He was also afraid of what he might find out. Was she married? Did she have kids? While a part of him was curious, he didn't want to be jealous, or in the doldrums.

Then there was the time he was watching a movie, and wanted me to watch it with him. It was a film of skiing, shot in the high mountain tops where the snow glistened virgin powder, unblemished by any ski tracks. It showed a single expert skier dropping from a helicopter onto a steep, smooth summit you'd think of as avalanche country, twisting his way down the slope, knee deep in plumes of jetting snow, taking jumps off cliffs with effortless flips and spins. Lee kept laughing, rubbing his hands, and exclaiming, "Better than sex! That is better than sex!"

All along the time Lee lived with me, he was doing his volunteer EMS work out in the streets, which was another of his loves. He would come home and tell me all the stories of how the time went, how the "save" was made. One time I asked him, "So, in all, about how many people do you think you have saved?"

"How many saves, how many losses?" He looked sad, then said, "I've only lost one. I was young, too enthusiastic. She stopped breathing, and I got scared. I started to do CPR on her, you know, where you push the diaphragm repetitively, alternating with blowing into the mouth while holding the nose pinched closed. And…" He hesitated, then continued as if divulging a secret, "And I broke every rib in her body and caused her heart to collapse." He looked away. That was all that mattered to him at that moment; the one he killed instead of the many he saved.

My heart went out to him. "It's O.K., Lee. She would have died anyway if you didn't try to save her."

No splash into his list of loves would be complete without the majesty of the Great Outdoors, and his knack for obtaining equipment, for free mind you. This gave him the privilege of enjoying nature to the max. He would decide what he wanted in terms of merchandise, scheme what to do with it, and then convince the manufacturer or store selling it to give it to him for free for "product testing." I know he received a couple of tents

LOVE

and a couple of sleeping bags that way. I believe that is also how Lee acquired his red sirocco kayak, nesting cook ware, and other camping equipment for his expedition down the Mississippi. His first December with me, he gained a bright orange, winter ready tent, yellow sleeping bag, and warm gloves, and set up camp in my back yard in the snow for his product testing. He couldn't have been happier, unless of course, you placed him in the mountains. Ahh! The good life, winter camping!

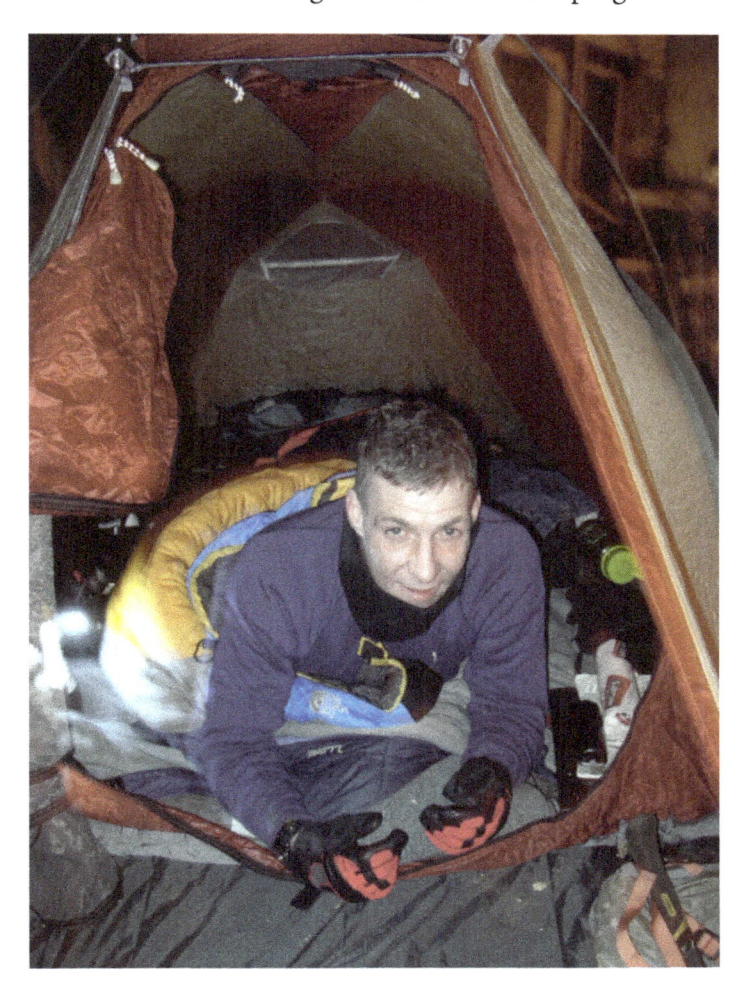

FRIENDS and ENEMIES

Lee was proud of his ability to get sponsorship for his Kayak racing. He would build a relationship with a company, and loved to get their decals and T-shirts. He pretty much wore only T-shirts with the names and logos of places that had sponsored him. He also made use of these relationships at other times. For instance, when the hurricane Katrina hit New Orleans, he made a deal with one outfitter, I believe it was Granite Gear, to send all kinds of equipment down there to help out—tents, backpacks, and with a different company for medical supplies.

Now Lee was out to get sponsorship for kayaking down the Mississippi River. He had approached the matter once before when he was going down the river alone, and had a friend, Bill, spotting him along the way. Bill would also meet him at the end of the day for camping and dinner. Basically, Bill footed the bill for the trip, and all the sponsors had to do was provide decals, T-shirts, and some equipment. Then Bill had a stroke, and the trip had to be discontinued. All this happened long before Lee moved in with me. Bill survived, but was almost totally paralyzed. His sister was the executor, and cleared Bill's house out of everything, including what belonged to Lee. Lee says he lost a lot because of her, thousands of dollars worth of equipment. She also "put Bill away," and it took Lee a long time to track him down. Lee was able to make himself executor instead of the sister, and was able to get Bill into a personal home where he could be as independent as possible. That is what Bill wanted. As Lee would put it, "that guy is 100% in the head and only 20% in the body." Bill had to learn to talk all over again, as well as to stand and to transfer by himself. Bill could answer "yes" and "no" easily, so that is how Lee communicated with him, by asking questions that could be answered "yes" or "no." Lee wasn't about to let his friend down. If you were a friend of Lee, he would make sure you were always taken care of. He'd often tell me, "I'd take a bullet for my friends," and, "I'll never let any of my friends get left behind." He said it frequently, and he meant it. I was glad to be counted a friend of Lee. I certainly wouldn't want to be his enemy, because he knew how to fight, too. Whether it was fisticuffs in the street, or fighting "the system" he almost always won.

And Lee did have his enemies. He thought it was because he did EMS work, which included taking needles away from street folk. I think it had to do with that "chip on his shoulder." I have been with him when a Somali man innocently asked him if he lost his leg in the military, and Lee got all hostile, yelled, would have hit the guy if I hadn't been there saying, "Come on Lee, let's go; COME ON!" I think Lee enjoyed proving himself. And he was prejudiced against Somalis.

One time shortly after moving in, Lee was shot in the back and left ankle with salt pellets. They just grazed his skin, but the channel from the one on his back went from just above his waist almost to his right shoulder. Lee said the person who shot him had been standing on a roof, and had the cowardliness to shoot Lee in the **back** when Lee was **walking away** after their spat. Lee couldn't run, because of his prosthetic, so the guy got two good shots at him. Lee was almost as upset about the cowardliness of being shot in the back as about being shot at all. The salt pellets stung like anything, and Lee had me flush out the channels with a washcloth and water. As I did it, his whole back twitched from the pain, but he made no sound.

I wouldn't let Lee have a gun in the house. He often argued with me that, "If a tank were coming down the alley shooting, you would want me to have a weapon;" "people like you rely on people like me for protection; you should let me have a gun and be glad!" He was a Lieutenant, after all, and showed me his Lieutenant bars. But I was firm. I don't believe in guns. I think they create more problems than they solve. They are dangerous, deadly dangerous, unnecessary when people can talk out their differences with diplomacy, and there is such a finality with guns. There is no going back to saying, "Oh, I found more information; I didn't want to kill you after all." And then there was the matter of my being schizoaffective. I didn't tell Lee this, but I was worried what *I* might do if there were a gun in the house. Though I was stable now, when I first had problems, I did try to commit suicide, and I was afraid of what I might do to myself or someone else.

I also took Lee to visit Bill sometimes, to save him taxi fare. I would drop him off, he would spend the day with Bill, then take a taxi home. They sometimes went to the McDonald's near Bill's home. It must have been a strange sight—a man with one artificial leg pushing another in a wheelchair. Sometimes they tooled around the neighborhood, or sat in the backyard where Bill lived with his caretakers.

Lee wanted Bill to be able to visit us and built a ramp over the back steps so sturdy and heavy I couldn't begin to lift it even though it was meant to be removable. It was so sturdy and heavy duty that when Joe accidentally drove a front wheel of his pick up, fully loaded with scrap metal, onto it, there was no damage. That is the kind of carpenter Lee was, making things so they would last.

Bill did come to visit more than once, also before the ramp was made. Bill liked being independent and would take the bus. Lee knew he was coming, but not exactly when, and Bill would surprise him. But Lee, always the gentleman to his friends, would walk Bill to the bus stop after the visit. Lee was always trying to get me and Bill to develop a friendship, too. While it never happened, Bill did bring some of his weaving books for me to look at, which were interesting. Lee also managed to get Bill to give me first one, and then another, of his precious weavings, precious because he was no longer able to weave. As therapy, Lee had used some of Bill's money to buy him a weaving frame, sewing machine, cloth to cut and sew, beads to intersperse, and a toy (yes, that is what the gadget is called) for winding the strands of cloth. But as much as Bill tried, he could not get his arms and hands to work the warp and woof, or even sew.

The rugs Bill gave me are beautiful. The first is in stripes of navy blue, green, blue-green, violet, and deep purple, hashed with threads of navy blue that ties the whole work of art together. These rugs are meant to be decorative, and Lee helped me hang this one on my dining room wall near the ceiling. The second rug is zigzag stripes of pink and white, with fringe. I had no more room on my walls to hang it, so I placed it under my wicker rocker where it could be seen well, and hopefully, protected.

Lee was an early riser. But he knew I was not. When he was well, he would wait until 8:15 AM and then call me, his cell phone to my land line. Although that phone did not have caller ID, I always knew it would be Lee, and he would make my day a little brighter by cheerily saying, "Good morning, Sunshine! How are you doing this morning!" Often his call would be what got me out of bed, or I would have slept longer. But he thought 8:15 AM was late enough. We would do some chatting, and then, if he needed meds, or wanted to see Bill, we would make arrangements for that. He never wanted to put me out, though, and on those rare occasions when I wanted to go back to bed, he would take a taxi.

Another good friend of Lee's during this period, and long before I ever met Lee, was Joe. Joe always wore blue denim overalls and, even into cold weather, flip-flops. He salvaged scrap metal from back alleys, and made a living at it. As you might guess, Joe's clothes were always covered with grease and grime from his occupation.

Joe and Lee were as tight as they come. They would do just about anything for each other. Joe had some of Lee's stuff stored in his rented locker. Joe would be needed transportation. Joe paid the food bill at times. Joe always came through, although he had an elderly mother he cared for, and she came first, before Joe could attend to Lee's needs. He was a very sweet, relaxed, easy going guy. In Lee's opinion, nothing could rile Joe.

From left to right: Lee, me, Joe

On the back of the picture, dated 11/14/15, Lee wrote:

> To Kathy,
> The older Sister & Brother I never had, kept me out of trouble, and allowed me to follow my dreams and be of service to others, Always Friends, Lee B.

March was the time when Lee would start getting together with his good fishing buddy, Freddie. They'd go out several times a season starting with the fishing opener, sometimes to a lake in Wisconsin, sometimes to the St. Croix River to do catch and release. They would make trips well into the summer. This was the summer of the "Big Mistake" that they laughed about long after, 'though at the time, it was nothing but a sore point between them, and cause of much argument. They managed to remember everything they needed to be on the lake—the boat, the hitch, the poles, the worms, the life jackets—everything except the paddles to maneuver the boat! They got all the way to the lake in Wisconsin and were unloading when they realized their mistake, had to pack up again, come all the way back to Minneapolis for the paddles, and set off on their adventure once more.

Lee on left, Freddie on right

Freddie was a tree trimmer by trade, and Lee would sometimes borrow tools from him to trim a tree in my backyard that overhung my parking pad (and my neighbor's garden). This year, however, the tree had a lot of dead wood up high, and Lee convinced me to hire Freddie to do a thorough job on it, not just let Lee cut low lying branches. Freddie came with a partner who climbed the tree to saw off branches. He had bid me the price of $100.00 for the whole tree, but didn't clean it completely, only as much as he thought reasonable for $100.00. I then agreed to pay him extra to have his helper return and finish the job.

Later, Lee and Freddie had a falling out of sorts, over racial prejudice, because, as Freddie put it, "Lee and I, we are both so stubborn." This had happened on a previous occasion as well, but they had made up because they thoroughly missed each other's company fishing. But this time, Freddie was so mad, he said he would not lend Lee tools any more, and he was done, done with their friendship for good. Lee was forlorn. He was sure Freddie meant it this time. Not only was he out a fishing buddy, he was out a defender and protector. Freddie was a feared Hell's Angels motorcycle gang member, and Lee often threatened to sic Freddie on trouble makers, or have him back Lee up in protecting Lee's friends. But it was the fishing Lee missed most; no fun to do alone, and besides, Lee didn't have a vehicle to get to a good fishing hole. He did ask me once if I wanted to go fishing, but I don't care for fishing.

Freddie was no one you would want to mess with. One day a guy was bad mouthing Freddie, so Freddie grabbed him by his non-dominant hand, lifted him up onto the hood of his car, and would have punched him out with his dominant hand except that a Black woman at the bus stop said, "Hey, this is better than Jerry Springer!" The guy was definitely shook up, and seemed to have learned his lesson, so Freddie left it at that. Since color seemed to play an important role in his story, I asked if the guy were White or Black, he said, "White." Then pointed to himself and said, "I am Colored," as he pulled down the neck of his shirt to reveal pale skin and tattoos. "$10,000 worth of tattoos," he smiled proudly. Yes, he was definitely strong. Freddie stored his 1000 pound Harley Davidson motorcycles in his basement, and would carry them up the stairs to use them. He was with Hell's Angels for five years. He has seen The Rocky Horror Picture Show three hundred times.

Freddie vehemently declares, "I prefer animals to people, and like good people more than assholes. I spend $150 per week for food for the birds and squirrels in the back yard, give carrots to the rabbits, and bring five apples for the deer at the dump every time I go there." He had a heart of gold towards his friends. As I mentioned before, he would lend Lee tools, and I recently found out that he gave away the front end of his favorite motorcycle to a friend whose bike needed repairs.

I had the honor and privilege to get a tour through part of Freddie's house one time. He has lived in it sixty nine years to date, I say honor and privilege, because the front of his house not only contained several traditional "no trespassing" signs, he had others that gave one an eerie stomach and hyper breath. They read "No Trespassing, Violators will be shot, Survivors will be shot again;" "You Haven't got a Prayer;" "I'd turn back if I were you;" "Bad Ass Mother Fucker;" and "Special Issue-Resident-Permanent, 2001-2050, USA Terrorist Hunting Permit, No Bag Limit-Tagging Not Required;" "Attention thieves, please carry your I.D. so next of kin can be notified;" and "Warning! No Stupid people beyond this point." As you might guess, Freddie keeps not one, but **many**, guns in his home, fully loaded and ready to fire at a moments notice.

The front of his house was captivating, giving a sense of the wild and spicy flavor of his character, and I had to stand a while admiring it. He had made up street signs, some given to him, that read things like "Jim Morrison Blvd;" "Haight Ashbury;" "Grateful Dead;" "Love Street;" "Dead Head Way;" "Biker Blvd;" "Abbey Road;" and "US route 66." He had car license plates made for Oregon and New York that read "Dead Head," and another that read: "You've got a friend in Dead Head Pennsylvania."

Freddie had plaques out front, some that you might expect, like pictures of Harley Davidson motorcycles and "Sturgis, Live the Legend" (a yearly, humongous motorcycle gathering in North Dakota), and others that are more political and visionary: "Was Columbus a Terrorist or an Illegal Alien?;" "Liberty and Justice for All, Offer Not Available in some areas, Prices subject to change;" "I can already sense you're going to be a major obstacle on my path to Enlightenment;" "To hell with what people think. Just be who you are and you'll be happy – Willie Nelson;" "Welcome friends and guests to Fisherman's Paradise;" "One Fine Fisherman lives here with the catch of his life;" "Remember – As far as anyone knows – We're a nice, normal family;" "It is dangerous to be right when the government is wrong;" the entire Pledge of Allegiance, the entire First Amendment to the Constitution of the United States of America; and "My Creed" by Dean Alfange, which is so Freddie that I include it here:

> I do not choose to be a common man. It is my right to be uncommon – if I can. I seek
> opportunity – not security. I do not wish to be a kept citizen, jumbled and dulled by
> having the state look after me.

I want to take the calculated risk; to dream and to
build, to fail and to succeed.

I refuse to barter incentive for a soul. I prefer the
challenges of life to the guaranteed
existence; the thrill of fulfillment to the stale calm of
utopia. I will not trade freedom
for beneficence, nor my dignity for a hand out. I will
never cower before any master nor
bend to any threat.

It is my heritage to stand erect, proud and unafraid;
to think and act for myself, enjoy
the benefits of my creations and to face the world
boldly and say, this I have done.

All this is what it means to be an American.

The interior of Freddie's house is quite dramatic. It is four levels, including basement, one and a half feet deep in "valuable belongings" with a narrow path in between. All the walls are coated ceiling to floor with posters (including sexy women), and bumper stickers, of which I will mention only one: "It doesn't require many words to speak the truth–Chief Joseph."

Lee had a couple other close friends, Steve B. and Steve T., who started coming around. Steve B. was a carpenter like Lee, and would sometimes give Lee work when he had contracts. He had returned to Minneapolis after living in Texas, and was starting life afresh. Steve T. was very religious and had a lot of illness in his family, and Lee did his best to be supportive with phone calls and visits. The two Steves were not friends of each other, however. Lee would have one or the other over. They were never over at the same time, and I did not get to know them well.

Lee was always having financial difficulties and took his **kayak** to the pawn shop. I didn't realize it was gone from the side of the house until a few days had passed, and when I saw it missing, I thought it had been stolen.

"No," he informed me, "I pawned it."

I was distraught. I knew he didn't do that lightly. He loved that kayak, and it was what he had planned to use to make another attempt at finishing the run of the Mississippi. It was his whole life prize and desire now lost. I could only guess how much that must have hurt, and I couldn't stand how much it hurt **ME** to see him in this predicament. Right away, before anyone else could, I went to the pawn shop and bought his kayak, for a mere $500. (Replacement value would have been four times that.) Then I gave it back to Lee as an early Christmas present. Lee was extremely grateful, to say the least, and he wanted me to name his kayak as a way of thanking me. I couldn't come up with any good names. That is when Lee hit upon the Odyssey. "Who is the guy in the Odyssey who makes a lifelong trip and comes back to find his wife still faithful to him? What is his wife's name?"

I looked it up in my dictionary, the one I got from my grandfather with his initials on the cover. "Odysseus was the man, and his wife who remained faithful all those years despite many suitors was named Penelope."

"That's it!" he said excitedly. "Penelope! I got her back! Penelope! Boats are always female."

After that, Lee started calling me "The Older Sister I Never Had;" he would refer to me that way when introducing me to people he knew or met, and would also talk about me that way in conversations I was not privy to.

Christmas came. It was one of the most fun Christmases I have ever had. I decorated my little four foot artificial tree that I inherited from my grandmother, and placed it on the dining room table. I put little presents under the tree, like chocolate bars and such, and every present was from "Santa Claus" with a short note detailing the qualities the person had demonstrated that made them worthy of receiving the present. I only remember a couple of the presents. One was a $50 gift card to Lee from Target, and the card pictured their mascot, Spot. After Lee opened that present, I told him, "That's the closest you'll get to having a dog in this house." I gave Andrew a $50 gift card to a major art store, Dick Blick. Lee also got a care package from his mom, with socks, and money, and other needed clothes. We had a great time, and Lee would often tell me after that, "That had to be about the best Christmas I ever had!"

But living with Lee continued to be problematic. Finally, on February 28, 2012, I wrote this letter to Lee:

To: Lee Blanchette
Re: 30 day notice

This letter is to inform you that you will be required to vacate the premises of 2108 Milwaukee Ave., Mpls,

MN 55404 by March 31, 2012, 5:00 pm. You are a wonderful person, but as a renter and house-mate, you have been very difficult and I no longer wish to live with you.

I will give you excellent references.
Sincerely, Kathleen I. Haskins

I believe he went to live at his Pastors house after that; I don't really remember. Nor do I remember what he did that made me allow him back in. All I know is, I have in my records another letter, dated April 14, 2012, that reads:

To: Lee Raymond Blanchette
Re: Continuing to live at 2108 Milwaukee Ave.

This letter is to certify that Lee Raymond Blanchette has been invited to continue living at 2108 Milwaukee Ave. because of steps he is taking to improve his stability, health, and life, and to certify that he has agreed to stay. The lease arrangement will be month to month, as it was earlier, but with the hopes that it will be a long term arrangement.

Signed,
Kathleen I Haskins
Loren Haskins
Thank you,
Respectfully,
Lee Blanchette

Denny stayed a night with us that summer; he was a bicyclist. No, I mean a **REAL** bicyclist. He did tour trips across the country and would write about his experiences. He had legs of iron (metaphorically). One of his first trips was from Fargo to Cleveland; he was planning to stay with a friend of his wife, Jane, but then Lee convinced him to stay with us, instead, saying he wasn't drinking anymore, and that he had a kayak race he wanted Denny to witness. The race never happened. But Denny had the pleasure of cycling the East Bank of the Mississippi River by himself, and then Lee took Denny to Minnehaha Falls, which he found memorable. Unfortunately, Denny caught Lee drinking on my back porch, and that was the end of that, although he and I hit it off. I told Denny he was always welcome to stay in our house any time he had another ride that passed our way. Denny confided in me, "Lee is really good hearted; he cares a lot about the people around him. He pulls up others around him. He just can't seem to pull up himself."

CAN DO!

Lee was very capable, and always busy. When he was not doing carpentry for someone, or working around my house, he would visit friends, listen to music on his phone, or play his guitar. He always watched "This Old House," which shows how to do home projects such as building garages or remodeling the kitchen, and he also regularly watched another program on how manufactured items are made. He was forever planning his upcoming trip down the Mississippi River, making notes, keeping a journal, and starting to write a book. The book was meant to include all of his life, but especially talk about his limb loss and how it affected him, and his journey down the Mississippi. He wanted his book to demonstrate that limb loss and limb difference is an inconvenience, not a handicap.

Paddling the Mississippi was his dream. Partly because he loved the water and boating so much, and partly because no amputee had ever done that before. People climbed mountains, or biked across the country as awesome goals, but he wanted to stand out from the crowd. He thought if he could be the first amputee to paddle the Mississippi, he could set an example for others with limb loss, limb difference, or even mental challenges. He wanted all people to live their dreams, to set powerful goals and assail the goals until they succeed. Lee believed in people. He had a "can do" attitude towards himself, and also towards others. He wanted people, particularly those with challenges, to know they could do anything they set their mind to.

He admitted to falling down a lot, but that was just part of the deal. His attitude was: you just get up and keep going. He learned how to adjust his "leg" so that it stayed in top performance. He kept in close contact with his prosthetic manager to make sure everything worked as it ought to. He had problems with the computer activation on his phone for the knee, but he took it all in stride. And he didn't let anything slow him down. He walked, did carpentry, snow shoveled, and biked like a maniac.

Lee did everything with passion. He talked with passion. He biked with passion. His bicycle was not just transportation, it was pure joy of speed and freedom. It took him to visit his friends, and get his hair cut. But mostly, he just plain liked being outside in the fresh air breezes and being as close to nature as he could get.

RHYTHM OF RIDES

By Kathy Haskins

Peddle to the push, plowing
his pulse forward and up,
surveying the path before
him with acute
eye, even as speeding
strongly, ramming his way through
the traffic strewn road, jeopardizing
his journey, in competition with cars,
he raced his way
from place to place.

BOAT YOUR VOTE

2012 was the year the "marriage amendment" was to be voted on in Minnesota; a vote **against** it meant you were for marriage allowed between same-sex persons. As I have known and liked a number of GLBTQ persons, particularly in my church, and think they should have every right to fall in love and get married like anyone else, (after all "Love is Love" as my church coined), I decided I wanted to do something big to help sway voters to vote against the amendment. Lee was ready to help me with that, because his friend, Bill, was gay. While Lee didn't understand how a guy could not like women, he was ready to accept his friend's feelings. So the two of us made plans for an event renting canoes on Lake Harriet to draw attention to the vote. However, that was going to be too costly, and we didn't have enough time to prepare for such an event, so we settled for an organized picnic in the park. Lee and I collaborated on making a poster, and then he was in charge of distributing them. He and I both approached musicians and spokespersons. I put an ad in City Pages, a free, local newspaper, and ordered lots of hamburger. It was a flop. The musicians showed, the speakers showed, but no one else came to our picnic except a few curious passersbys.

Change of venue: Boat Your Vote for Equal Marriage now Picnic in the Park at Minnehaha

Unfortunately, due to the expense and lack of time allotted for preparation of the Lake Harriet event Boat Your Vote for Equal Marriage has been cancelled. However, the good news is that the venue has been changed to a Picnic in the Park in opposition to the marriage amendment and will now be held at *Minnehaha Park*.

PICNIC IN THE PARK OPPOSING THE MARRIAGE AMENDMENT

On Saturday, July 14, 2012 bring your picnic basket with dishes and your blanket to the Minnehaha Park pergola area from the hours of 10:00am to 4:00pm. Free hot dogs and hamburgers will be available thanks to a discount by Brothers Meat and Seafood. Thanks also to Seward Co-op for their gift certificate making possible free vegan burgers. All are welcome for an afternoon of sharing pleasant conversation with other people regarding the topic of opposition to the marriage amendment. Enjoy live acoustic music from various local artists, guest speakers, and open mic presentations. We will also have information tables including voter registration and rainbow flags. FYI there is a nominal fee for parking. In the event of inclement weather, all activities will be held in the public pavilion adjacent to the restaurant "Sea Salt" at Minnehaha Falls. For more information, contact :

Lee Blanchette or Kathy Haskins at (612)305-0940

TOO COMFORTABLE

Lee also refinished my front porch, back deck, and the upper deck off his room that has a tall railing around it, with an outdoor varnish. It was quite a big job, and I was so grateful to Lee. I was working four days a week at the time, and it kept raining when I wanted to do the job myself. Then here was Lee, looking for work, and free on the dry days! His doing the rail of the upper deck was the most helpful, because I would have had to get a two story ladder, and move it little by little as I worked my way around the exterior, whereas Lee was so tall, he could just stand on his deck, lean over the railing to get the exterior of the spindles, then later get the rest of the spindles and rail top. He had to do it his way, though, which meant sanding first. It came out nice, but I wanted, and got, a couple of coats of varnish on to protect the wood.

Squirrel watching attracted Lee as a pastime on his porch. The critters would vault between the Box Elder and the Mulberry tree. They would chase each other viciously, eat leaf buds in the spring, and mulberries late summer. Lee named the most bold ones Tic and Tac; I don't know if he could tell them apart. A leafy squirrel nest rigged in the uppermost branches of the Box Elder seemed to be home sweet home. When the young squirrels emerged, their antics were erratic as they, too, learned to leap from swaying limb to bowing branch.

I feel forever blessed with good luck, because in the twenty five years of my living at this address, there has always been an albino Grey Squirrel living in the neighborhood. The gene expression is very strong. Sometimes there is one that lives two blocks south of me. Sometimes the blood line springs north, across busy Franklin Avenue. Yet, there is always one in the vicinity. I even have had one living in my back yard a couple of years.

We also have a plethora of white tailed rabbits in my yard, munching spring, summer, and fall on the field of violets growing there (too shady for grass). But in the winter, they favor the bark of my purple lilac bushes. I had three gorgeous bushes in my backyard that they stripped of bark the entire circumference as high as they could reach. Naturally, they killed the lilacs completely. Those cute bunnies similarly devoured much of the bark of the sweeping line of lilacs at the front of my house, killing many stems. It saddened me. I love lilacs. Oh well. I also love bunnies.

But there was only so much time Lee wanted to spend watching squirrels, bunnies and birds, and spying on the occasional neighbors skirting through the alley. Lee really wanted a computer. He hemmed and hawed, then came out and asked me if I would get him a cheap one. He suggested we go to the pawn shop to look for one as there are always good deals there. I said yes, I am willing to go to look at any rate. The pawn shop had a surprising array of computers at reasonable prices. I didn't want to get him a piece of junk, though, so we took our time looking over the lap tops and their installed software. Finally, I hit upon one that I liked. Lee thought it must be worth $1,000. It was selling for $450. I thought a moment about the person who must have given it up; would he/she ever have the resources to reclaim it? It was the only one that looked like a reliable, well outfitted computer. We took it. And Lee had another of his friends help him "scrub" it down. I was so glad to have gotten it for him. He used that computer constantly.

All spring, it seemed like I wasn't making any cash; although I got tips, my fanny pack never seemed to reflect it. It never occurred to me that one of my housemates might be lifting money from fanny pack. I trusted them both. Lee was losing a lot of weight, and I found out he was dumpster diving for food. Andrew was a student with a loan and plenty of money of his own. I also had a wallet that I took to work in my back pocket because we were not to have obvious money holders, like purses, at work; they look like you are asking for a tip, and officially, mine was a non tip job. I always maintained an exact amount of money in exact bills in my wallet. Andrew was out of town when I found a $5.00 bill missing from my wallet. There was no question that it had to be Lee, and I figured it was he who had been keeping my fanny pack trim, too, although I did not accuse him of that. I only approached him about the $5.00 dollar bill. He was cornered, and admitted to taking it to buy some whiskey, but said that was all he ever took. I realized I couldn't trust Lee any more, and decided to give him the boot once again.

August 6, 2012, I wrote this letter to Lee.

Dear Lee,

I regret to inform you that I must ask you to move out of the house at 2108 Milwaukee Ave per our conversation this morning. I feel great loss, as I like you very much and have enjoyed you as a housemate. I wish you luck and gook times in the future.

As the first of the month is already past, I will give you until September 30 at noon to leave. This gives you almost two months to find new housing. If you find something sooner than that, I will pro-rate the rent for you. I will NOT extend the stay permitted past September 30. Lots of places come available this time of year, and you may be able to find housing cheaper than mine, if you look.

Take care of yourself,
Kathleen Haskins

MISSION LODGE

Lee was so upset with himself and the whole incident, that he put himself into Mission Lodge sober house in Plymouth, about ten miles away. I must admit, I had come to write Lee off as a looser and a charity case. But time tempered that. I learned to respect him—especially after he set his heart on becoming sober. And he was so skilled. He knew lots about most everything, could fix most anything, could build absolutely anything of wood in the most sturdy manner. He knew roofing, though was leery to do it anymore because of instability on his "leg." Still, he climbed ladders to clean downspouts and gutters, or to knock icicles off the roof. He could work with concrete, could do plumbing better that the experts. He knew all the building standards and codes, and would surpass them. He would slide the top of window well covers under siding for a seal that refused to allow rain to slip through the seam into the basement.

Lee had a code of ethics and honor, and while he had stolen from me, he had done so with aplomb, taking only what he needed as base necessity, even braving to eat from garbage cans, losing forty pounds that he could ill afford, before he chose to filch my excess. He left me plenty to get by on my own. (I had an earlier roomie clean me out of all my cash, so I felt lucky.) In a sense, Lee could rationalize it; I had money and he didn't. But I wish he had come and spelled out how bad he found his situation and asked for help. It is never justified to steal.

When he elected to enter Mission Lodge, he asked me if I would send him a care package now and then. I knew how much he liked care packages, so I agreed. Every month, around the middle of the month, I would send him a care package. Always included were two packs of Camel 99 filters, his cigarette of choice. Usually I would include a large bag of Jolly Ranchers (his favorite candy) and a couple of packages of Grandma's brand cookies. If I was feeling really ambitious, I would bake him a couple dozen cookies, which he always shared, either chocolate chip or peanut butter, his two favorite—especially the peanut butter ones. In the middle of winter, I sent him wool socks in the mix; once I included two pair new pants; his prosthetic was constantly wearing holes in his pants. Once I included a hardcover book, "Voices in the Ocean: A journey into the wild and haunting world of dolphins," by Susan Casey which I read myself before sending it to him. One of the things I gave him, he later gave back to me to let me know the feelings were mutual—a refrigerator magnet with an old saying on it: "Good friends are like stars. You don't always see them, but you know they're always there...." And when I would get a $2.00 bill as a tip, I would send him that for good luck.

His first month at Mission, he was not allowed to leave the premises, but after that, he made a habit of taking the van into town and visiting people. When it snowed, I could always count on him coming in and shoveling me out. He was a God send. He knew I thought that way, too, and he always made sure I was the first person he took care of before shoveling out other friends and clients. He often brought me a gift when he came. He had become friends with a Native American at Mission Lodge who knew how to do beading and make jewelry. Lee first had this friend make me a choker out of small shells, white disks with a hint of blue on them. I loved it so much that Lee had him make me beaded earrings of blue, white, and black resembling eagle feathers. Another gift I appreciate and use constantly is one of those credit card holders that prevent surreptitious copying of your number and other info. As a metaphorical gift, he gave me a pure white, ceramic bell with a kneeling cherub on top, telling me I was his guardian angel. Even not having money, he could come up with the best gifts.

Lee rigged his bicycle especially for his "leg." He would frequently ride it into Minneapolis, because of the freedom it gave him in deciding when to return to Mission. He could bike those ten miles as fast as a car could go.

And Mission Lodge was very good for Lee. They started out by having him make a plan for sobriety, and when he would reach one goal, they would have him make another goal. He made friends with the staff, particularly the administrator, Dan. They had a wood workshop that Lee enjoyed working in. Lee made Dan a new desk; made the office a new medicine cabinet; made a double hung bench swing for the front yard, all solid as a rock. He helped in keeping the premises clean, and did his prescribed chores.

As part of one of his plans, he wrote me the following letter. His honor meant never apologizing for any of his actions. On the rare occasions when he would admit to a mistake it was for him an epiphany that altered him for good.

6/2/13

My Dearest Kathy (Sis)

Finally in complete confidence I can sit here without second guessing, what it has taken me a long time to first come to terms with what it is I am apologizing about and why. Please accept not only this letter, in hand I'm writing, but my actions that in the past year not only surprised me but surpassed the expectation of many. But my sincere apology for the inexcusable action of stealing money from you, to support my drinking. I am very sorry, and I know about forgiveness and how it works. But the violation of trust has been brought out and this is something I don't take lightly, and I know it's one of your principal values you live by. I hope in time, you can once again bring yourself to not only forgive me, but learn how to trust me once again. Please keep in mind that I am fully aware of your thoughts and feelings. I've given considerable time and thought on how I was to address this issue and not it only it be embarrassing, and shameful, but it's the first step in addressing my alcoholism, this being taking full responsibility for my actions. It has been some time now. And you have been truly the Older Sister I never had. Even though there are a few that have come close, but there's hands down for a small person you are truly the bigger sis, not only in heart, but in friendship and kindness. The world should have more people such as yourself in it. A lot of things would be resolved without incident. Nothing but Peace and Harmony. Also I really don't know where to begin when it comes to two other issues in my life that has been one constant battle after another. We both have had many of a long discussion. One of which has in all efforts, allowed me to move forward, you know. And have encouraged me to facilitate a much more meaningful mother son relationship with my mother. And the other related issues around it. I know that without your support both financial, moral. Note: I did not forget about Dan at Mission lodge and how he allowed me the much needed time off. Anyway you made a difficult issue a little easier. I can honestly say, with conviction, I've done my part. And continue to do so. Thank you!! But most importantly your continued friendship has allowed me the opportunity to acquire some much needed improvements to my prosthetic. (That's still in the breaking in process) My time here at Mission being in a sober environment, utilizing services made available without being another Hennepin County Methadone consumer.

Sincerely,
Lee

Lee was adamant about not getting on Methadone, because it is so addictive. A person on Methadone has no life, no freedom; they are tied to the doctor and office that dispenses it in order to get their fix every day. The only difference between Methadone and street drugs, according to Lee, is that

Methadone is prescribed by a doctor and has a consistent formula. It won't be cut with things like Fentanyl, which makes Heroin so unpredictable and a cause of deaths. Methadone is the pain killer of choice of seemingly all doctors, and Lee fought hard to be put on other medications instead, and when he won out, he received continued support from the doctor by voluntarily reducing the dosage he used. Thus, he was able to **have** a life, go biking, do carpentry, shovel snow, whatever!

As part of his fight to not be on Methadone, and also to get improvements to his prosthesis, Lee was assigned a social worker. She had a box of documents about Lee in her car that became stolen. Neither the administration at Mission Lodge, nor this social worker did much about it, and his identity was stolen. Lee had to work out all the details by himself in getting a new, identity—contacting the bank, social security, Hennepin County, doctors and all. It was a mess. Lee was "pissed," and said, "Nobody will fight for me. I am so damn tired of fighting for myself. I am done! DONE!" The ramifications lasted a long time. But eventually, matters cleared up, and he was back to being as cheerful as ever.

As I said, Lee got a lot out of being at Mission Lodge. He, and the administration, thought he was ready to leave, and get an apartment of his own. After some looking, Lee did find a place, the whole first floor of a duplex for $350 per month with six month lease. O.K., so it wasn't in the best of neighborhoods, but it was right on the edge with better neighborhood, and it was near bus transportation, and it was within walking distance of my house. He had the first month rent and deposit, but the landlord also wanted last month rent in advance, and Lee didn't have that much money. It looked like a real good deal, and the landlord seemed good, too, so I agreed to pay the last month advance. Lee was overjoyed. He had not had this much space to himself ever before, and he made good use of it, but keeping it sparse and clean. He always was a very clean, tidy, and well organized person. Once set up, he had me come see his digs, so he could show it off. He wanted my approval. He showed me some buckshot that he had found in the carpeting, a reminder of the kind of neighborhood he was living in. I again advised him not to get a gun of his own, saying it would likely only make trouble for him. He asked if I would keep his kayak for him so it didn't get stolen or damaged where he was living. I agreed. And I knew it would be very hard on Lee to be on his own and stay sober, so I told him, "Be sure to call me any time if you need someone to talk to, day or night, no matter the time, 1:00 AM, 2:00 AM, anything. Know that I am here for you." And he took me up on it. Not every day, but often. Midnight or 1:00 AM was the usual, and after about an hour or so, I would say something like, "This has been a good talk, Lee. I am glad you called. Can I go back to bed now?"

Lee did some work for that landlord as well, clearing out the basement, fixing the cement steps, and fixing the back screen door. Both the landlord and Lee thought they had made good deals. Among the things that Lee found in the basement while clearing it out was an old, dirty, broken music box. Lee spent hours and hours on that music box, cleaning it, and fixing it so it would play again. Then he gave it to me as a present, in gratitude of all I had done for him. This was a labor of love, a true gift from the heart, and I cherish it immensely for that reason as well as because it was such a nice gift. It is a small, metal oval-shaped box with delicate legs, floral engravings on the sides and also framing a picture on the top of a seated Victorian girl dressed in blue and white. The tune is "Duh, duh, duh...just like me, they long to be, close to you." He denied that the song had any special message; it just happened to be the one on the music box. But I loved it anyway. I just happen to like that song. He had given me gifts before for my knick knack collection—a pair of blue, ceramic dolphins, leaping; a clear glass whale; a blue glass Blue Bird, Easter Bunny families in their egg houses, a seated mermaid candlestick holder—but the music box was uniquely exquisite, delightful, and "me."

Over that winter, I was glad he lived relatively close to me. He would come shovel me out, just as he did last winter. Of course I paid him. But that he made the effort *I* thought was above and beyond; he was still almost a mile away. He was always like that, going above and beyond for his friends. And he knew I hated to shovel. He also shoveled the whole side of the block where he lived, and for certain persons in my neighborhood with whom he had become friends while living with me. He enjoyed being outside, enjoyed being active, enjoyed doing things for others, and frequently would shovel friends out for free. He had incredible amounts of energy, would often be up by 4:00 AM and in bed by 10:00 PM, getting only six hours of sleep. He would run himself ragged, working several days in a row, then have to take several days off to heal.

But this duplex was not to become a long term solution for Lee. The people upstairs had a kid who would run around, and the pounding overhead got to Lee. More importantly, the couple would get into yelling spats in the middle of the night that would disturb Lee's sleep. And then, there were all those needles he would find in the alley. It was just plain a dangerous, unpleasant, place to live, even if he had a nice space. So, when his lease was up in March, he moved, again not far from me, but into better, though still not good, neighborhood. This time, he had a basement apartment in a fourplex. He brought his kayak along with him, and it made for a nice conversation piece. In the apartment, he started to paint a mural on one of the walls of dolphins and other sea life. But this apartment was riddled with bed bugs. We could watch them climb down the wall from the upper apartment like a waterfall. Even after the building was sprayed for them, they came back in droves. And Lee was so bored. He tried so hard to stay sober, but with nothing to do, he started drinking again, which he felt guilty about. The final straw, though, was one night when he was sitting on the steps to the upper apartments smoking and minding his own business, a chap came along and pointed a gun at Lee, asking for money. Lee managed to talk him down, but was so riled that he didn't want to live there anymore. So, he asked me to take the kayak back, and he put himself back in Mission Lodge sober house.

Lee had to start all over again, square one. He became a support teacher in the wood shop, showing other clients how to soak and bend wood, and to use the technique to make oval and round jewelry boxes, one of which he gave to me. He took on the administration for the way they handed out medications. He made use of the opportunity to get another upgrade to his "leg." Gratefully, medicine had made some advances, and it was at this time Lee was able to be cured of hepatitis C. It was a real hassle. But, most importantly, he got himself sober again.

And he continued to come into town. He really got around, was so curious and friendly that he was able to get work that way. The neighborhood bicycle shop had hired someone to paint a mural on the exterior of their building with a scene of a bike path going past park and town through the four seasons. Lee not only was able to talk his way into helping out, he obtained permission to paint an image of himself in the "autumn" panel—a dude with a bicycle and a prosthetic leg on the right side. He also started to talk about going back to school to learn sign language, and try signing as a profession, where his "leg" wouldn't be such a liability.

Lee used some of the money he earned to buy a dolphin. It was almost a foot long, and made of solid black walnut wood. The grain in it was incredibly beautiful, and it was carved in a diving position. It cost Lee over $50, more than he normally would spend on anything, but he really wanted this dolphin badly, and prized it after he got possession of it. He brought it to my house for safe keeping, making sure I understood this was not one of his many presents to me, but remained his. I was just to safeguard it so it would not get broken. A few days later, though, he was back again to pick it up. He liked it so much he didn't want to be without it. Not long after that, he was back again with the walnut dolphin—broken. Fin and tail re-glued on, and humbly asked me to watch over it again for him.

On one of Lee's visits to my house during this time, he noticed that the spray hose on my kitchen sink was very weak. I had a plumber fix the entire faucet earlier, and that was the best the plumber was able to do with the spray hose. Lee thought it was pathetic. He was no plumber, but he was sure he could make it spray well and strong. He got under the sink, cut and reconnected the tubing. It was amazing how well it worked after that. Lee was like that; he knew a lot about lots of things, enough to fix about anything.

RIVER RUN

Denny's trips just made Lee want to make another try at the Mississippi River all the more, starting where he left off in Minneapolis. In April 2014, Lee got permission to take leave of Mission Lodge without losing his place or bed. He contacted sponsors again for decals and shirts, but mostly was going to foot the bill on his social security check. As I had been storing a lot of Lee's important papers, my dining room table got a lot of use. Only one end by me for eating; the other end was piled with Lee's papers and maps. Not road maps—he did not have a car—but nautical maps of the whole length of the Mississippi. He would pour over his maps hours on end, planning the route for his next adventure. He wanted me to be as excited about it as he was. "I'll put in here, and this lock and dam will be the first I'll go through. Then I'll make it to open water where the barges are. That is where it really gets dangerous, because the barges have a hard time seeing you. Also, their wakes can overturn a kayak if you're not careful."

Lee wasn't leaving anything to chance. He made me his point of contact, and loaded me with all the information I would need in case he never came back, whether because of death, or because he might decide to stay in New Orleans and not come back. He connected me with his banker, giving me her phone number and the address of the bank, also gave me the routing number and checking account number so I could make direct deposits to checking if need be, also his debit card # and pin #. He updated his phone so that payments would be made automatically every month, and gave me all the numbers I might need in case something malfunctioned with that—carrier #, serial #, account #, phone # to store, and activation date. He gave me his computer password and e-mail. He gave me his medical payer #, medical ID and group #'s, social security # and date of birth. He gave me all the information for Winkley Orthotics and Prosthetics, including address, phone # and fax #, manager's name and e-mail who worked on him, and the serial # for the bionic leg and activation pin # for it. He gave me the name, address and phone # of his primary care doctor. He gave me the make of the kayak, its registration #, and the expiration date of the registration. He gave me his blood type, the codes for his locking briefcases, his medication list, and a short will: if he died, he wanted to be cremated, and his ashes strewn into the Mississippi River, with half being mailed back to next of kin or strewn in the Atlantic Ocean. He wanted his nephew, Joey, to get his tools, and his "leg" and leg parts to go back to Winkley. He made out a health care directive.

Lee made it to the Mississippi with his kayak and all his gear. He would call me at the end of each day to say where he was and how he was doing. He loved passing by the bluffs, very beautiful, reaching up, up, up, until they kissed the sky. The cliffs were topped with green trees of every variety and hue, a flamboyant crew cut. The river rippled and bubbled frothily with long plumes of sun sparkling waves. The freedom of being out there on the murky water, in nature, simultaneously domesticated yet wild, was exhilarating. Always on the lookout for wildlife where forested shore sloped down to the river's edge, and the occasional sandy beach, he once witnessed a doe drinking. All around were the sounds of birds chirping away, the paddles dipping a swirling cadence, the trees chattering serenade in the leafy breeze.

He felt so small going through locks meant for barges with their tugs, and was gratified that the lock and dam lockmasters would raise and lower the water just for him. He marveled how the tiny tugs could manipulate the huge, heavy barges. One day he had to fight the wind hard, but he enjoyed getting into the rhythm of the challenge and feeling his muscles work. Another day, he had to cross the river in order to find a campsite, a difficult and dangerous experience. Then Lee didn't call. I got worried and filed a "missing person" report.

He was expecting to arrive in Davenport that night, but the Davenport police hadn't seen him, nor had the DNR. The army corps of engineers at lock and dam # 12 at Belleview above Davenport had not seen a red kayak come through, nor at lock and dam # 11 in Dubuque above that. Finally Lee called from the little town of Cassville, above Dubuque. He had capsized far from shore, but managed to swim to shore without losing his kayak or any of his gear; his "leg" was strapped down to the kayak, so it was saved as well. But he was violently ill from the river water, both from swimming in it and because he had been drinking it, using a filter that apparently was not good enough. He had been lying on the beach, hallucinating and vomiting, and would have died right there except for a Good Samaritan who came along and took Lee and his gear to a flop house where he could get some treatment and recover.

The people at the flop house were very good to Lee. They took him to the doctor for medication to treat the bacteria he had become infected with, and they set up a bed for him in the hallway. Once Lee got better, they promised to hold onto Lee's kayak and gear for him until next year so he could make another attempt at the river starting from Cassville. I wired Lee $300 so he could pay for the bus ticket home.

Lee's adventure continued on the Greyhound bus. In the station was a young girl who reminded Lee of his sister, April, in that she was a special needs person. She was traveling alone, and Lee was angry, angry at her family for letting her travel alone, angry at the bus station for not providing her with an escort. Bus stations can be dangerous places; you don't know what kind of hoodlums you'll meet there, ready to take advantage of an innocent girl. In the end, he bought a ticket for Chicago, and escorted the girl that far himself, before returning to Minneapolis. When Lee finally returned home and told me the story, he would say he'd repay me when he could, and I would always reply, "Don't worry about it; I am just glad to have you home alive," knowing he didn't have the money, and would probably pawn something else of value to get it to me, like his beloved guitar. Alas, another trip was not to be; a tornado hit Cassville, leveled the whole town, and all Lee's gear was lost, including the kayak.

MOM

Lee's mom was proud that he had graduated from Outward Bound, and she sent him a copy of the newspaper article she had cut out when he was a boy, along with some pictures, to my house. It helped Lee realize that his mom had always been there for him, even when he was turning her away. He had told me that they were just too much alike, hard headed and argumentative, and that is why they never got along. But after his mom sent the article and pictures and things, I said to Lee, "See! She does love you and think of you!" Lee started calling his mom every once in a while. It almost always ended in argument, but at least he tried. One time I talked to Georgia, and told her how much the article and pictures meant. She was glad, and then confided to me that the real problem between them was his drinking. She knew how hard it would be for him to stop, because she used to overindulge herself, and now that she had stopped, she realized how important it was especially for alcoholics to refrain from drinking. His continued drinking was the major topic of their arguments. But Lee needed his mom's love and approval even as much as if he were still a child.

At times, I served as a surrogate Mom, too. Whenever Lee received something special, he would give it to me "to save for him." He had a carpenter's belt buckle, and a coast guard belt buckle that he placed in my kitchen window for me to take care of, and then to that he added a fire department decal, a toy dump truck with a rock in its bed, and a black Winkley Orthotics and Prosthetics mug. He had placed them in the window while he was living with me. When he later moved from my house to Mission Lodge sober house, not only did he leave those with me, he would send me the certificates of "Congratulations, three months sober!" "Congratulations, six months sober!" "Congratulations, nine months sober!" to hold on to, and probably also to prove to me of his progress.

Lee wanted his mom, dad, and sister, April, to come to Minneapolis and meet his tried and true buddies—Joe, Bill, and me. Eventually they did, as they heard Lee became successful in sobriety again, and they wanted to be supportive. Lee wanted to take his family and us to the Himalayan Restaurant, as he and I knew the owners there, and Lee had done some work for them repairing an entry door jam. I told him I would pay so that he could take us there. But Lee's dad, Danny, snuck to the registrar and paid before I could. It was so nice meeting them. Danny was fairly quiet, while Georgia and April kept us entertained. The picture of Lee, me, and Joe comes from that restaurant visit.

After Danny, Georgia, and April came visiting, Lee became much closer to them; he was always close to April. According to Lee, "April thinks I walk on water!" But he also became worried about the three of them. Danny and Georgia were getting older now, and April was a special needs adult. April wasn't supposed to live past her teen years, but now was in her late thirties. Lee kept trying to reach out to his younger brother, Mark, about how the two of them should make plans to care for the other three as time went on and they aged. But Mark wouldn't return Lee's calls. Lee became rather desperate "to go home" to see his brother to make plans before it was too late, and he wanted to see his mom again badly. He had it in his mind that she was in danger of dying soon, and he wanted to be there for her and prevent it if possible. He asked me if I would finance his way home, but I was not ready to do that again; I had done it once before while he was living with me. Besides, his mom had seemed relatively healthy for her age when his family had visited. He couldn't get anyone else to pay his way either.

It was like a premonition he had. Georgia died just over a year later, on December 18, 2016 of cerebral hemorrhaging. Lee was inconsolable. "If only I had been there…," he would say over and over again, "I would have seen the signs and gotten her help. Maybe she would still be alive if I had gone home." His family did pay Lee's way to go to the funeral, and Lee was grateful for that, but he couldn't forgive himself for not being able to get there while she was still alive.

At Lee's suggestion, the family planted a rose bush at their home in memory of Georgia. Then, once Lee returned, he created two memorial gardens for his mom, one behind Seward Café, where he planted a Maple seedling and a variety of flowers, and one underneath my Box Elder employing a rescued sapling having oval, maroon leaves, and surrounding it with blue and yellow pansies. But he was still unsuccessful at connecting with his brother Mark on how they should care for Danny and April.

HOMELESS

It was spring of 2018, and Lee became obsessed with not living at Mission Lodge any more. I couldn't quite tell if they had tossed him out, or if he truly was that sick of living with drug addicts who were constantly backsliding (junkies and tweekers, as he called them). I would not let him move back into my house, even to flop on the couch for a while. His pastor was done with living with him also, but had a van that he sold to Lee for a dollar to live in. For a while, Lee was parking it on the street, and moving it every day so as not to be found out. But that got old fast, and he was afraid of being found out, because it is illegal to sleep in your vehicle on the street. He asked me if he could just park his van in my drive over night while he was sleeping, and that he would take it away during the day while he was looking for housing. I concurred. We had space, as I was the only one with a vehicle (that my parents helped me get), and there was room for two, side by side. And so it went for a couple of months. When he arrived in the evening, it was usually after dark, and no one knew he had arrived. He also usually was gone with the sunrise before anyone had gotten up. He was very aware that he was not welcome because of his history of stealing and of drinking.

One day when I went out back to get in my car and run errands, I noticed that his van was still there, with the back hatch up, and I saw him laid out sleeping, sort of. I took a closer look to make sure he was O.K. He assured me he was; he just hadn't gotten much sleep that night because someone was wandering the alley in the middle of the night and had tried to break into his van. He never did get a good night's sleep, needing to "always sleep with one eye open," as he told me. He showed off his van, how he had rigged it up with a plywood sleeping platform about fifteen inches off the floor, and slid all his boxes and crates of tools underneath. He had a foam pad and blankets to pad the plywood, and of course, his beloved sleeping bag to sleep in. (He always slept in his sleeping bag, even when he lived in my house.) We talked about his sobriety. He said he had been sober ever since getting the van, that he took very seriously the need to not drink while driving, or even having an empty, open bottle in his possession. He was proud to be responsible about not dirtying my yard, either, and pointed out a large, black, plastic box hidden in the bushes, that he had been using as a toilet. That is when the request came.

"I do need to use the toilet, and it is midday. May I use the one in your house?"

"Of course!" I replied. "You needn't go to those extremes. I'll give you a key to the house for using the bathroom. And if you want to shower in the morning, too, you can do that as well." I knew how important it was to him to have his morning "shit, shower, and shave," and felt guilty for denying him that.

"I won't trouble you for a shower, I get those elsewhere. But I would greatly appreciate access to the biffy," he said.

And so, as the days grew longer, Lee began to come home before dark, and would tell me how his day went. He got himself a case worker, Will, from Avivo, to help him in the search for housing. They were not having much luck. Lee really wanted an apartment of his own, again, but Will was pressing for another sober house.

"I just gotta break this guy in," Lee told me on more than one occasion.

As he did with everyone in his life, Lee brought Will by our house to introduce him to me. You've got to remember, Lee was still living in his van. So they were carrying out business in the front seats of the van when I walked out the door to go to work. Will finally did start looking for apartments, but they were unaffordable because Lee refused to live in bad neighborhood again. When that proved unproductive, Lee agreed to looking at roommate situations, though wasn't happy about it. Everyone seemed to want an application fee, and that was becoming expensive, too.

Then a breakthrough. Will found him a situation like mine, where the landlady lived on premises. After speaking with her by phone, Lee thought it would work out, and they set up an in-person interview. Lee was excited and talked of little else all week. But afterwards brought great disappointment.

"You know that house, roommate situation like here, that Will found for me? Well, it is a fuckin' drug house! That landlady, seemed so sweet, has a guy in there who smokes marijuana! And she says anybody who moves in must be fine with that; he is not moving out. I could never live there! Being around him, and all his smoke, it would jeopardize my EMS! They would test me for drugs, and I would show positive, and I would never be able to get a license!" Lee was down in the dumps. "I guess it is up to me to find a place to live. It always comes down to that, me fighting my own battles. I am so sick of fighting."

Despite his struggle to find housing, Lee did other big projects that summer, too. Always looking for a way to make a buck, he asked what he could do around the house. I said he could pull up the 2 by 4's that made my raised bed garden—they were looking very shabby. It turned out to be a much bigger project than either of us realized. He ended up cutting out the screen, stapled from porch to boards, which had been keeping the mice out. Then he turned over the whole garden so that it was dirt—I had wanted the plants left; they were "Snow on the Mountain," that do very well in shade, and spread well. He could not tell them from the weeds. I was upset, and he got all huffy. "I am not a landscaper!" he blurted. "But I'll fix it; I'll make it a rock garden, and then you won't have to worry about any weeds." He pinned down landscape fabric, and "borrowed" a huge trough and shovel from a river rock wholesaler, and got the rock at wholesale pricing. Brought it in his van. It did look good when he was finished. The trough he left for the trash pick-up, and the shovel he left in our basement. "They won't miss them, they have so much stuff, and it is a blasted long way to go just to return them!"

The whole summer long, while Lee was looking for housing, he was also working as a volunteer EMS at "tent city." Tent city started out as a couple of homeless families tenting it along the Hiawatha corridor near Franklin Ave East where there was a little ribbon of public land. Soon, more homeless families joined them, and it wasn't long before there were more than 100 families squeezed into the tiny width of land. Businesses donated tents and cooking supplies. A porta-potty appeared. Police were stationed there to make sure things didn't get out of hand. Lee would go there to treat wounds, and drug overdoses. He would come home raving about how the police did nothing; they just stood around talking to each other. It was up to Lee, as a citizen volunteer, to do the work of getting involved. Afterwards, he would most often come in while I was making dinner. He would walk in and stretch out his arms for a hug. "I did good today," he would say. I would go over to the door and give him a hug. He would hug me gently, having learned I did not like being squeezed with his strength. He would tell me how many people he "saved" that day, ie. treated with Narcan, and of the people he persuaded to not use, at least for that day.

One day he came in looking quite proud of himself. "She'll live. Her arm is so scarred up with needle marks, they are probably going to have to amputate her arm. But she'll live. I called the ambulance to take her to the hospital."

Another time, he came in all in a flurry, rushed over to me, knelt on his prosthetic, and kissed the back of my hand, saying, "It is so good to know that you are here."

I didn't know how to respond. "What are you doing? What happened?"

"I lost one today." Now he put his cheek on my hand.

"I am so sorry."

"He just didn't come through. I'm done. I can't do this anymore."

I was silent.

"I need a break," he continued. "I'm going up North for a while. Maybe a few days or more. Don't worry about me."

Well, what do you know, a few days later I got a call from Lee. He was in the Anoka county jail. "I don't have much time to talk, so just listen. Call all my friends and tell them where I am, and call Will and tell him to get his ass up here NOW. I'll explain everything later." He gave me his prisoner number.

He had been caught red handed, an open bottle in his van. He says he was parked in a campground, but that doesn't matter. In jail, they took his leg away from him, saying it could be used as a weapon. They gave him a wheelchair to tool around in. Will and Joe were good about visiting him. I did not visit him even once.

Will was great, got Lee a lawyer, and Lee was out on parole in a month. After getting out, Lee complained that they didn't have the decency to let him keep his leg. So much time in the wheelchair had caused all his muscles to atrophy to the point that he had great difficulty walking. He did finally get his walking back, but he had to work long and hard at it. In the mean time, he was staying in a halfway house, River Place Counseling Center, as a requirement for getting out of prison. He had to go to their programs and obey all their other sobriety rules. When his time was up at River Place, he requested I come get his stuff and store it in my house for him, which I did. It was probably a twenty mile trip one way. He showed me the community room before I left. So, Lee was left searching for more long term housing again. He ended up in yet another sober house, not Mission Lodge, which is one reason I thought they may have required him to leave.

REDEMPTION

In the mean time, I had a room open up in my house. I was not about to let Lee move in, though. One of the people who answered my ad was a woman in her thirties named Carrie Anne, and her nine year old boy. We seemed to have a lot in common like eating healthy, organic food, and she had a very up-beat personality. Lee warned me not to rent to her. "She'll be a problem!" he said. If she wants to live in the same room with her boy, and can't afford a separate room for him, they'll be a problem!"

I didn't listen to Lee. She was on assistance, and above board with that she could just afford one room. She and her son had bunk beds, so I stored my bed in the basement. I dropped my client who had bed bug problems in his building (and an occasional bug in his apartment) just for her. It was probably a good idea anyway. Carrie Anne had me sign a note stipulating that her signature on the lease was "only binding provided that a pest management professional determined that this address is free of bed bugs, or until this address has been treated and they have been eradicated." I contacted a bed bug professional who used dogs to sniff them out, and they assured me a dog can smell one or two bugs. I wrote a note to my two current housemates; "K9 detection tomorrow, Tuesday, 9:00 a.m. All areas must be free of food, breakables such as glasses, nothing with scent, **no cooking for twelve hours prior**, garbage out, no candles/air fresheners. Leave bedding on and technician will remove—must have no smells that will compete with bed bug odor. No cleaning until after dog is here." The dog found no bed bugs. I had them come through again, because I saw what I thought was a bed bug nest between the panes of my bedroom window. It turned out to be that a paper wasp had started making a nest, and the technician was able to retrieve the piece of paper. It was exactly like toilet paper, and the technician was sure it was toilet paper, only our toilet paper had a butterfly pattern on it, and this was plain.

I gave Carrie Anne and her son little welcome presents, which they both liked a lot. Initially, we all got on well. Carrie Anne referred to me and my home as their "room of requirement," a reference to the Harry Potter series in which there was a room in the old castle/school that would become whatever you wanted it to be. She started having car problems, and I would give her rides for groceries, and to the bank while her car was being fixed.

Then problems did start to develop. Carrie Anne kinda' took over the kitchen. She was there almost constantly preparing food for herself and her son, and she did not like having anyone else in the kitchen while she was there. She would make him a breakfast of bagels, and then carrot slices, sandwich, cookie and chips for lunch, then drive him to school two periods late, because, by that time, he would have missed the bus. At nine years, he still did not know how to toast a bagel, put cream cheese on it, sprinkle it with a little cinnamon, and press on raisins. She did everything for him.

More problems developed when Carrie Anne noticed some black mold growing inside an access panel behind the shower in the upstairs bathroom. When I said that I would clean it up, she became hysterical. "No, don't touch it! If you do, the spores will go throughout the house! It needs to be done by a professional, and they need to be able to see it to know how to treat it." I put a piece of packing tape over it so the spores couldn't escape, and so you could see through. She also wanted the basement remediated, for there was a little white mold on a few of the overhead beams. I started calling mold remediation experts, but not quickly enough for Carrie Anne.

We four had a very nice Christmas; Carrie Anne's parents bought us a very nice, full, three foot wide tree to decorate. Then, Carrie Anne went all out for her son, buying him all kinds of tech. equipment. No wonder they had been skimping on food for so long. And the other housemate, Equayja, bought us adults electric massagers. No one let on that anything was amiss. But, like, the day after we celebrated Christmas, Carrie Anne left me a message that she and her son were having a "sleepover" at a friend's house. All their stuff was here. Finally, after a week, I called her to find out what was going on. They had moved in with some friends. She informed me they had a month to remove their belongings, even though they were not paying rent, because the mold was a health issue. Soon, she was saying that she and her son could not move back in because of allergies to mold and the mold would always be there even once the house was remediated. Thank goodness. She would be breaking the lease (for health reasons, which made it permissible), but I did not want her and her son around any longer.

Very fortuitously, I met Chris, of World Effort Foundation, who offered me a ride one day when I was running after my bus and missed it. Even though I had a car, I always took the bus or light rail downtown because parking is so hard to come by and so expensive there. When Chris off-handedly offered his help in other ways than giving me a ride, I told him of my problems with Carrie Anne, and asked if he knew of anywhere she could move. He made some suggestions, then said he had a small moving van belonging to World Effort Foundation that we could borrow to move her. I thanked him gratefully, and promised World Effort Foundation $500 for the use of their truck and some helpers. I called Carrie Anne and told her of the "free" moving truck and of efforts I had been making to find storage for her belongings. Luckily, she had been making arrangements for storage, and for friends to come help with the move.

Lee also came to the rescue; came down from up north to help with the move, and was able to rope some of his friends into joining us as well. Turned out, he and Chris knew each other from an earlier time when Lee had stayed at Days Inn. Lee had nothing but praise for Chris, and said how lucky I was to run into him. Between Carrie Anne's friends, and Lee and his friends, I thankfully had a lot of help.

Carrie Anne sat out in her car in the driveway, wearing a chemical toxins respirator, directing the move by phone. She said she couldn't come in because of the mold. The process took most of three days, because she wanted everything wiped down with vinegar, then dried with clean, new paper towel AS it was going out the door. This is in the dead of winter, mind you. Her mattress she wanted tossed; it was torn. But her son's mattress she wanted saved—again by taking the old mattress cover off and putting a new one on AS it was going out the door. Lee got really mad at Carrie Anne for putting us all through such a comedy, and told her off. Said he would call the police if she ever came back after her things were out.

Lee came by frequently the next few days, to "see how I was faring." I found out he was looking for housing once again. Someone in this new sober house stole from him, so rather than make a scene, he was just going to move out. He didn't know where to turn. He no longer had a car to live in. Mission Lodge was not an option. I asked my other housemate, Equayja, if she would mind if Lee stayed in the open room just for the month of February while he looked for more permanent housing, and I got the house remediated of mold in preparation of obtaining a new housemate. I felt an obligation to Lee; he had done so much to get rid of Carrie Anne and her son. And also, he truly seemed to have matured over the course of events. He wasn't cursing so much. And he was taking full responsibility for his jail time. He was walking away from troublesome situations instead of starting fights. Equayja agreed. She was quiet and stayed in her room most of the time anyway.

Around this time, Lee got a job removing snow with a real outfit. Sometimes he used a snow blower, and sometimes he had the privilege of running a snow plow. He'd do church parking lots, and the sidewalks of certain businesses. Nor did he forget me and his friends. He ran himself ragged, pushing himself until he was ready to drop, the "leg" no longer being able to take the punishment of the cold and pressure.

Once, when he was in the snow plow, he plowed the half of my parking pad next to my car. It was a little space for a plow, and he accidentally backed into my car as he was leaving. My poor car, my awesome car. Even though the dent was pretty big and unsightly, it didn't do much structural damage. It was partly on the front door, partly on the front side above the axle. He missed the wheel. The door still worked perfectly, and so did the window and lock. No problem. He asked me if I wanted him to fix it. I said no, not necessary, but how about fixing the rust spots starting just above my rear wheels on both sides in exchange. He was afraid he could not match the paint, so I asked him to paint flowers there instead. At first he was resistant, thinking it would look funny and make my car hard to sell, if I ever wanted to do that. But then he got into the idea, and started planning a vine going up each side of the back, with flowers and leaves all along the winding vine. It sounded fine, until he told me how he would do it, and that the job would only last a few years. Whoa, this was getting out of hand. I nixed the idea, and asked him to just go back to a simple repair job, even if the paint didn't match. He was disappointed; he had put so much thought into the process. But then agreed; a simple fix was probably best.

My friendship with Lee grew. He knew he was walking on eggshells, and he didn't want to blow it. He would get up early, and spend most of the day every day either on the computer looking for housing or at Avivo looking for housing. Then in the evening we would chat. I was letting him stay the month of February for free so he could save up and have the first month rent and deposit somewhere. The week before the end of February, Lee was quite depressed. He hadn't been able to find anything in his price range, not apartments, not roommate situations, not sober housing. And he had used up most of the money he was supposed to be saving.

"I'm not going to live on the streets," he stressed, "I'll put a bullet though my head before I do that!" I saw that he was serious. Not looking at me, he continued, "I'll pay you $600 per month rent (his total Social Security Disability check) and quit smoking and drinking if you let me live here." It took all his guts to get it out.

I was ready to cry, seeing him so torn up and on edge. "That won't be necessary, Lee." I tried to remain calm. "You know rent is only $500 per month here, but I would like you to quit drinking and quit smoking if you are going to stay on. I know you can do it. Think how long you were sober at Mission Lodge. Three years, was it?"

He removed a necklace from around his neck, and kissed it. Then he gave it to me, saying, "You just saved my life. I was a goner, all done fighting. Now this is for you. An Indian woman gave it to me when I saved the life of her boy."

I looked at it. It was a round pendent. Around the top in Italian I could make out something about Holy Joseph, and below was a figure of a seated Joseph holding the Christ child in his lap, a potted lily on the left, a dove near Joseph's other shoulder, a staff, and what looked like a rifle on the right. "Thanks, Lee, I will cherish it." I put it on. And from that day forward, even now, I wear it every day, taking it off only at night to sleep. It is a big responsibility, having the power of life or death over someone. That must be the feeling Lee has every time he uses Narcan and saves someone from OD-ing.

There is an old Jewish saying, "Save one life, you have saved the whole world." I mused on that saying. I only saved one life, Lee's. But Lee was saving lives over and over again! How many times over had he saved the world?! Both Jews and Christians are taught to "love your God with all your heart, with all your soul, with all your mind, and with all your might," and to "love your neighbor as yourself." I tried to live this way, but Lee lived this commitment with total passion, and an adorable innocence that was at the same time worldly. He was no Saint, but, like his sister, April, thought, he walked on water.

All the time Equayja had been at my place, I had been having problems with her over "stinky stuff" she was using. It smelled to me like a bitter marijuana, but she insisted it wasn't, that I was just smelling essential oils, or a wax that she burned. She knew I would turn her out if she was using marijuana, because that was one of my specific interview questions, and it also stated in the lease that renters could not use illicit drugs. She would make her face look so innocent when she said it was not marijuana that she played me along for a long time. But it smelled so bad. Finally, I sat her down and said, "I don't care what it is that you are using, it smells really bad, and it stinks up the whole hallway and even comes into my room. You aren't going to be here forever. You will want to move when you leave school, or when your lease is up, or some other time. Let's just agree that you won't use that stinky stuff anymore while you live here, and you can go back to using it once you move out." She just looked down at her hands, and didn't say anything.

She stopped using for a while, but then she was back at it, stuffing clothing in the crack under her door in the hope that would prevent the stench from escaping. It only helped a little.

Lee thought she was using marijuana also, but didn't want to be the one responsible for her getting kicked out. So he would vacillate between agreeing with me, and saying I needed to give her the benefit of the doubt. When I had the mold remediation done, I also had a fan put in the bathroom to prevent the reoccurrence of the mold problem. That is when my bath towel started smelling like the bitter stinky stuff. Lee thought Equayja must be smoking in the bathroom, and turning on the fan to draw the smoke out. But he would not stand by me in confronting her. That is about the time I left on vacation for sunny San Diego to be with my family, and had the opportunity to smell what I was **told** was marijuana, and it was **exactly** like Equayja's stinky stuff. When I got back, I told Equayja in no uncertain terms that I knew she was using marijuana, and that her lying to me was even as upsetting as the use of it. I gave her until the end of May to find a new place to move to. Her lease was up, now on a month by month basis, so all I had to do was request her to leave; I didn't need to evict her.

Before I had put up any ads for Equayja's room, Lee asked me if he could move over to that room when she moved out. "Of course," I responded, "If you want to bother moving all your belongings over!"

"Definitely," was his assertion. "It will be easy to move my stuff; I don't have that much, and I really like that room." It was his old room, the one with the "tree house" deck.

"Sure, then. It's a deal. I just need to make sure her room gets cleaned out first."

Equyja waited until the very last day of May to move out, saying she still had no place to go to after a month and a half of looking, and that she was storing her belongings at her boyfriend's. She gave me no forwarding address, not to her boyfriend here, nor to her parents in New York. So I had no way to forward her mail, or send her a "Certificate of Rent Paid" form. For the longest time, we were getting letters for her from the Department of Corrections in New York—apparently she had been busted for drug use in New York. When I had asked her about the letters when they first appeared in the fall, Equayja had told me they had to do with child benefits from a previous, no good boyfriend, and her kid was living with her parents while she was in school. She could lie like Br'er Rabbit himself in the "Tar Baby," and I was the gullible fool.

It was like night and day. Lee had matured so much from the time he had lived with me earlier. He made a heroic effort to stop smoking. He tried all the tricks to quit smoking—nicotine gum, patches, easing off, and even tried going cold turkey for a while. But he became so irritable without his "smokes" that I begged him to go back to it. He made a compromise, not wanting to let me down on his quitting. He would take a couple of puffs, put the cigarette out, and replace it in the pack.

He really did stop drinking. The combination of less smoking and complete sobriety made him very pleasant to be around. He stopped using foul language around me, saving it for the street life. Just to test the waters, he went back to Palmer's, and let them know he had given up alcohol for good. Would they let him in, order a soda, and join the Hootenannies? They did.

A few nights later, he was triaging drug addicts at the Franklin Ave light rail station when he noticed the sign at the Caboose bar across the street. His favorite band was playing. Lee became down in the dumps. Here he was, doing his volunteer work conscientiously when he could be having fun. Oh well, the band would be too expensive for him anyway, as it was a big name. Lee came home, and then went back on the off chance he could get in for the second set. He had been sound person for them at one time. Not only did they let him in, they greeted him warmly, and didn't make him pay a dime. They wanted him to drink with them, but he told them he was sticking to his sobriety. Because of his commitment, he had a great time.

SIAMESE FIGHTING FISH

In March, when I had given Lee his lease, he had renewed hope and love of life. One day, shortly after having been accepted, he asked me, "I know you won't let me get a dog, but how about a fish? Can I have a fish?" Immediately I said, "Of course!" Unlike a dog, a fish would not have large ongoing expenses, and needs.

"I'd like a Siamese Fighting Fish! They are so cool. They have to be kept in a bowl by themselves or they will attack other fish, and tear each other to pieces. I love their bright colors and feathery fins. Can I have two? To keep each other company—in separate bowls of course? That way they stay active, blowing bubbles and raising their fins at each other in aggression." He was a little boy again, who had been promised the most desirable treat ever, well, next to a brand new little puppy.

Two days later, when I had off work, we went to Aqua Land, a fish store where Lee knew the owners. Lee chatted with the owner a while, and told him we were here for Siamese Fighting

Fish. The three of us went to the display, in a prominent place, tiny containers all stacked one on top of another. Lee chose a feisty blue fish, "Hey there, Rocky, Rocky man!" and I chose an equally active red one per his request. I couldn't stand the thought of putting the fish in the small containers meant for Siamese Fighting Fish, so we got two, larger, Goldfish bowls, a net, and colorful gravel. I wanted plants, too, to give the fish a place to hide, make their bowl seem bigger with more places to go, and just plain to beautify each bowl. The owner convinced us to get bamboo, and plastic grasses, as we were not experienced with plant aquariums. Lee also got a little glass statue of 2 dolphins with gold snouts and fins about the size of his Siamese Fighting Fish to put in his bowl, and I got a larger orange and white "Nimo" for the bowl I was decorating. (The blue fish took to the dolphins once introduced to the tank, but the red fish was scared of huge Nimo.) Then we got dried Bloodworms for food for the fish, and the owner said to give each fish only three worms in the morning and again in the evening; that would be enough food, would keep them at peak activity levels, and would prevent the water from forming algae. The directions included using spring water (NOT tap water, as it was chlorinated, and NOT filtered water, as it didn't have needed micronutrients), and having the water at room temperature. Then we needed to let the fish acclimate in their bags to the water for one half hour before release. When changing water, we should not take out more than a fifth at a time. In all it came to just over $100.

"I will cover this, Lee, and you can help with future purchases of food and water. O.K?" He was relieved.

Simple? Well, we managed to botch it. First, there was still some ice on the ground; it was a very cold day, too. So when I went to the store for water, it seemed too cold for the fish after being in the car; I briefly heated each gallon of water in the microwave—just ten seconds until it was barely warm. Uh oh. Later found out that room temperature water is pretty darn cool. Then I put Lee in charge.

"The red one is yours!" He informed me.

"O.K., but you take care of it for me, alright?" I replied. "That way there won't be any problems in double feeding or anything else, and you know how to care for fish."

He floated the fish in their respective bowls, but when I passed the bowls only fifteen minutes later, he had already released them.

"Lee! What have you done! You know you were supposed to wait a half an hour!"

"It will be O.K. Fighting fish are very strong. They can endure most anything." he replied.

Both fish looked more lethargic than when they were in the store.

That evening, Lee called his dad and sister in Connecticut. "Guess what? I've got fish, Siamese Fighting Fish! The blue one is mine; his name is Rocky. April, how 'bout you name the red one."

She named him "Star."

Eventually, Rocky and Star made a comeback as their water cooled down. They started surfacing and blowing bubbles, and rippling their spiny, decorative fins, just as Lee had said they would.

"Hey, Rocky, hey, Spitfire! How you doing in there!" Lee would call out to the fish as he fed them.

"I thought the red one was Star; you let your sister name him."

"Spitfire is more appropriate though, don't you think?" he replied.

Lee was so enthusiastic about having the fish that he over cared for them, changing their water frequently, and about two-thirds of a tank at a time. Each time, the fish would become slow moving, lethargic, and hang out at the bottom of their bowls, or in their plastic grass. He also gave them a full pinch of bloodworms each, both morning and evening because he "didn't want them to go hungry." It just made the fish sluggish, and the water dirty faster.

Star/Spitfire never bounced back as quickly as Rocky. Lee blamed it on my having chosen an "old" fish; I attributed it to my having "cooked" the poor fish on its initial entry into our house. His water had been slightly warmer than Rocky's. The fish lived on a desk by the north window in the hallway. Lee started hanging a cloth in the window at night, thinking the cold nights might be causing their ill health. I got into the habit of checking on them every time I passed by to go to the bathroom. One day, I saw Star/Spitfire lying on the bottom of his bowl. Usually when he was in a funk like that, a tap on the glass would make him surface. This day, however it did not. Star/Spitfire was dead.

That did not stop Lee from feeling well, though. He still had Rocky, with whom he identified. And he was getting work. The Seward Café hired him to help with their clean-up, doing things like securing all locks at entry and egress points, fixing their gate, removing the ice freezer from the shop, breaking down the dumpsters, back yard clean-up, and other miscellaneous things. So he was making good money. He did a lot of extras around my house like doing yard work, buying new window well covers, and moving Carrie Anne's mattress to where it would be picked up by the trash.

SONGS HE WROTE

Lee started writing songs again. He particularly adored love songs, especially the heart break ones. This is an example of his writing:

D minor 3   A minor 7   F minor   G minor 7
Bridge over C minor?   Lead with open E flat?

Tear drop from your eye
Don't want you but
I need you

Love, It's like the river
Forever, the stars shine
Bright in your heart

I know you're thinking
of me tonight.

Question, in the moment
what it is in the
time.

Tonight becomes tomorrow
the drops in your eyes.

      Lee Blanchette
      3/23/19

Lee was churning out songs like crazy:

C major 7   D major   C major
F major   G   D major

There is only one
    She wants you
Blue in the sky
    (Left it in a letter)
I see it in your eyes…
    Tears, in the night
Then your Heart said goodbye
    (Left it in a letter)
Love you sent. Didn't
    Meant something to you
Believe in
    Blue Sky
There is only one
    I see it in your eyes.
Then your Heart said …
    Goodbye
    (Left it in a letter)

Blue in the sky, it
  Meant something to
Believe in.
  Heard said
Goodbye

  Lee Blanchette
  5/1/19

One more example: 5/1/19

You're steppin' along the
River side
With nothing left to lose
With nothing left to
Hide.

Rain drops fallen on
Your face.
There is nothing left
To replace.

A soft wind comes over
Me, and my eyes
Remember, the soft
Touch, of your warm
Embrace.

  Lee Blanchette

FALLING OFF THE WAGON

This particular spring was also the time when training would be held for EMS. Lee was so excited! Now he could get a license and be a real EMS, instead of just a volunteer! They only had training every other year for the EMS, so it was important to get it this year. The training was very expensive, so Lee was trying all kinds of tactics to figure out how to pay for it, like borrowing from his dad, and pulling favors from his uncle. The training was also in Montana, and he would need to go there—would I hold his room for him? How could he pay rent in two places, on top of the training fee?

And then disaster struck. He would have taken out a loan from a bank. However, he missed the deadline for filing by just a week! ***Just a week***! He was so overwrought the evening he found out, that he bought himself some whiskey, and oh, did he get ever so drunk. I knew it was inevitable. He had put so much at stake in this. He stayed downstairs and howled all night like a coyote at the moon, and sang boisterously, more off key than I could have imagined possible. It made for a long night, but in the morning I just laughed it off.

"Lee, you were so drunk last night!"

"I wasn't drunk!" then, looking at my smirk, "O.K. So I was drunk. I'll move out."

"You needn't do that."

"I'll move out, I say!"

"Don't Lee," I said more kindly. "I knew it had to happen. You had put so much stake into going to the training, I knew you must get drunk to survive. I'm giving you a second chance. Please take it. I enjoy having you around here. Please stay. Just because you fell off the wagon once doesn't mean it has to stay that way. You can pick yourself up and start all over again being sober. Let by-gones be by-gones."

He not only took me up on staying, he began drinking again. Not hard, but would mix whiskey in his Poweraid, thought he could hide it from me. He was not getting drunk, so I didn't say anything. Maybe I should have, but I didn't want him to move out. Finally, during a conversation we were having with Denny on the phone, I mentioned that Lee had gone back to drinking. Denny lit into Lee big time, "How could you do that to Kathy, Lee, when she has been so good to you and given you a second chance! Doesn't that mean anything to you? Do you want to end up like one of the drunks living under a bridge? Because that is where you are headed if you keep this up!"

Lee listened to him for almost half an hour, then hung up, mad. He would not call Denny to chat after that for about a month. But the conversation did get Lee to swear off drinking for good. May 14, 2019 was his first day of lasting sobriety. Lee could hold a grudge, and he held one against Denny for giving him "an ass chewing." But he missed his frequent conversations with Denny. And when I corrected Lee, and said, "No, Denny was not calling you a drunk, living in a cardboard box, under a bridge. He was just saying that that is the way you are headed unless you stay sober." When I said that, Lee took it as an opportunity to call Denny and make amends.

JUSTIN AND SKY

I got the middle bedroom rented out for the first of June, but luckily, the next renter didn't need to move in right away. I wanted holes in the wall patched up and the room re-painted first. Lee got a friend of his, Charlie, to do it. Both Charlie and I thought Lee was going to be doing it, too, so the work would go fast and they would have each other's company. But Lee bowed out, saying he wasn't a painter, but a carpenter. Charlie was a good sport about it, and finished the job.

It was June 6, 2019 when Justin and his dog, Sky, moved in. I am sure Lee was wondering why I would let Justin in with a dog, but not let him have a dog. Lee never seemed to understand that getting a dog was a serious commitment, like having a child; you had to be able to care for it—pay to feed it, pay vet bills, walk it daily at least once or twice, have stable work so you could continue to pay expenses, have a good place to live that accepts dogs, and be stable yourself, not bopping from one housing situation to another. Dogs don't go to sober houses. You don't want to have to give up your dog because you can't stay sober, or because you cannot afford it, or because you cannot find housing with it. It is a nice sentiment to say, "The dog would eat before me," but Lee could not even keep himself fed. He relied on his friend Joe, and sometimes me, to get him some food so he wouldn't starve. And as far as housing…!

Justin was just plain a nice guy, quiet and reserved, with a quirky, sarcastic sense of humor when he wasn't being serious. Ahh! The whiff of sizzling strips of yellow onion, melding flavors with sweet red bell pepper, baby Bok Choy, broccoli and cauliflower florets, tender zucchini, ripe tomatoes or curry and coconut milk, triangles of firm tofu, two bold cloves garlic, and don't forget the jalapeño pepper, whose spicy sting to the eyes makes you sneeze! That is how Justin cooked all the time. Well, O.K., not all the time, but enough; Justin is vegan.

His dog, Sky, was nothing short of awesome. He was a 10 year old German Sheppard mix. His coloring was exactly that of a German Sheppard, but the tips of his ears bent over, lending him a quizzical expression, and his face was a little more full. Sky knew the boundaries of the yard even though it wasn't fenced, and for the most part, would stick within them for doing his "business" while let out alone, then come right back for his "treat" of a dog biscuit. He had the vocabulary of a four year old. O.K., maybe a verbose two year old, and could differentiate when the same word was used for different meanings. He would tell you when he needed to go out by whining at the door. He would let you know when it was past feeding time or when he wanted a walk by hanging around and getting excited if you stood up, and was very quiet as far as "talking" goes. He never barked at other dogs, or at strangers coming in, 'though strangers might get a "roo-roo" greeting combined with a bouncy tail wagging. We let him get up on our two couches, even though he had a dog bed, and he spent his time going from one to another, if he wasn't on the rope outside in the sunshine.

Lee was very respectful of Justin as owner of the dog, and didn't get involved much at first. But as time went on, and it was O.K. with Justin, Lee would take Sky for occasional walks around the neighborhood, as would I. Sky was so good, he wouldn't pull at all on the leash. Justin was a fast walker, and Sky liked to walk fast with him. I walk slowly and the dog would stop, sniff, bound ahead a couple of steps, then feeling the slightest tension on his leash, he would look back at me like "Aw, Ma!" and would slow down to my pace again. I am sure he was just as good for Lee, who also didn't walk fast because of his prosthetic. Lee got to calling Sky "The dog who thought he was a cat," because Sky would so often be found rubbing his face or body along a couch. Sky particularly loved to do this if someone was petting him.

Then there was the day that Lee brought a homeless woman home and wanted permission to let her stay the night. It floored me. He was forever telling me of the extent he would go, walking different routes home to make sure he was not followed. Also, how he would never bring a homeless person home. But here it was, the situation arose. After a little pleading by Lee, I gave in, but seeing I wasn't whole heartedly for it, the woman said she would go elsewhere to a woman's shelter she knew of. It was about a two mile walk from my house. Lee convinced us both that I should take her there in my car since she had a big bag. I was much more ready to do that, and so she finally agreed; she didn't want to put us out.

After we dropped her off, Lee changed the radio station on my dash, and then turned the volume up unbearably loud. "Lee!" I yelled, "Turn that thing down! You're hurting my ears, and I can't concentrate on my driving!" Lee just snickered and turned it up more. I pulled over, really mad. I was about to tell him he could walk all the way home, but then realized that would be unfair, much harder on him than on a person with two legs, and his stump might get rubbed raw again. I turned the music down, and commanded, "You must keep the volume down! I'll let you listen to the stations you want to listen to, but if you are going to ride with me you must keep the volume down!"

SICK AGAIN

And then Lee contracted Shingles. It was a horrible case of it—raw welts under his left arm and over his tender, left breast, wider than, and longer than, fingers. It also appeared as puss covered, round red sores all over his back, particularly on the left side. It was very painful, and Lee was laid up for at least a month with it. His doctor gave him an ointment for it, which Lee would put everywhere he could reach, and then he would have me apply it to his back. His skin would quiver as I applied it, making me think of the time he had been shot with salt pellets. I of course did very careful hand washing, both before and after. I wanted to make sure I neither spread it, nor contracted it myself. I think I was more careful than Lee, and he was the one who was suffering. That was pretty much all I saw of Lee that June and July; he just stayed in his room, miserable, unless he was seeing his doctor. A sign of how miserable and out of it he felt was his beloved Rocky. Lee had Rocky on a desk shelf in the southern window. One day on entering Lee's room to help him, I realized the water was all green and full of algae. Lee had not been tending to the bowl he was so miserable. I walked over to the bowl to see how Rocky was fairing. He was on the bottom, on his side. I tapped the glass. No response. "It looks like Rocky is dead, too, now," I said, sorrowfully. Lee was unhappy about Rocky, but was suffering so much physically that he just winced, and asked to have the cream applied.

All July I am fidgety on account of Lee's illness, and I start writing:

SWELTERING SUMMER SQUAL
                By Kathy Haskins

> I am so sticky, sweaty, this
> summer, swinging my legs over the side of my bed,
> that the sheets smothering my skin peel
> away slowly as I stand.
> Careful am I to first surmise
> that the Sheppard is not beneath
> my feet. Two nights ago, he flopped the full night
> long along the foot of my bed on the floor,
> fearful of the thunderstorm. What a wakening!
> Rain drops driving ribbons
> against my window with wrath!
> Rattling the pains. Sky,
> you can calm down, cutie pie. I pet him
> pensively, riveted. Sky, have you come
> to me for comfort? Indeed. In earnest.
> His eyes plead. His body trembles.
> Slight of sleep, my reward;
> his soft fur in my fingers.
> I look out the window
> to the sky; yes, you can calm down now.

Lee was barely over the Shingles when he got Foot Drop, couldn't bend his foot up at all! He was advised to get a cane, or use crutches, but he couldn't see himself using either one. So, using his medical knowledge, he treated himself, with warm baths and gentle exercise. Every couple days would bring improvement, and it gave him great pleasure to show off the little gains in flexibility. In about six weeks, he was back to normal, hopping all over the place when he was not wearing his "leg."

The whole time Lee was convalescing and hibernating, I tried to cheer him up by making frequent runs (two or three times a week), to the corner gas station for cigarettes, white chocolate peanut butter cups, and grape Poweraid, things he seemed to live on. I would also make the twenty mile round trip trek to his pharmacy at his doctor's clinic weekly, sometimes with Lee, and sometimes by myself. Lee didn't like my driving; I was too cautious for his taste. He was used to driving fast with Freddie (nick named Fast Freddie for a reason). After some argument, we made peace—I would drive the way I like and feel safe driving, and he would shut up and just listen to his music on his head phones. I wanted to make sure he knew he was not alone, that people cared, and all he had to do was reach out.

Lee needed to go to the doctor every week to obtain his medication because he lived on strong pain killers. As his pharmacy was so far away, it was becoming quite expensive to take taxi cabs there and back. When I offered to take him for free, he didn't tarry long before he took me up on it. He had so little money, and when he did have a few extra dollars, he liked to go visit Bill, or give a few bucks to a homeless person.

SICK AGAIN

Lee was very generous. He had a hard time budgeting or holding on to money. He would get his social security check on the first of the month and it would be gone in just a few days. Rent, a food shopping, and then he had to last two or three weeks living on next to nothing. When not sick, he was scrambling for odd jobs here and there to make ends meet. Whenever he had a couple of extra dollars, it likely would go to a homeless person. It exasperated me that he would let go of his money so freely when he needed it for himself, but he saw it differently. Lee understood what it was to be hard up first hand, could really put himself in their place, and gave, not out of pity, but out of empathy. Occasionally, I would lend Lee money so he could buy cigarettes, candy, or a sandwich. He always repaid me what he borrowed.

As the summer drew to a close, Lee refinished the back upper and lower decks again. I was trying, unsuccessfully, to get someone out to rebuild my front porch. The contractor I was in contact with kept putting me off. Always there, Lee kept saying he could do it. September came, lots of rain, and it was almost too cold to apply coats of finish after rebuilding the porch, but I gave Lee the go ahead. I had to let him do it his way, or it wouldn't be done at all, even if the project was started. So after almost running afoul with trying to tell him how to do a procedure, I apologized, kept my mouth shut, and let him do it his way. In fact, he was very ingenious, leveling my porch roof that had a slight slant to it, propping up a corner of the porch under a pillar, and jacking the pillars up one at a time while pulling and laying the porch. This he did instead of using slanting poles to hold up the porch roof that a passerby could kick down and do damage to the house. It came out very nice, and all the neighbors admired his work.

During this time that Lee was well, he was still doing EMS volunteer work, mostly in the evenings. But he was becoming a little leery of continuing, saying he had a premonition something bad was going to happen. Drugs were rampant at a couple of the neighborhood stores, and there were gang beatings and guns showing up at the gas station. Lee was sure that if he continued, he would be shot. He made his rounds anyway, true to his path of "to strive to serve and not to yield." He would take needles away from the addicts. At first, the fire department allowed him to dispose of the needles there, for he had made himself a friend of the fire fighters and thought of himself as one of them. But Lee collected so many needles that they closed that avenue of disposal, and he started just dumping them in garbage cans. He wore heavy leather gloves when collecting the needles, but that didn't keep him from getting pricked by one at long last. When he got pricked, he was so worried what would happen. He got sick, and went to the doctor. He wouldn't talk about it much, and cloistered himself in his room again. All December he was sick, and I could hear him coughing hoarsely.

SANTA CLAUS

Christmas came. I wanted to make it special. I had met a real, live, "Santa" in early December at Common Ground Meditation Center during meditation, and immediately got the idea of having him come to our home and tell the stories surrounding Saint Nicolas and hand out presents Christmas Day. He was all for it as long as it wasn't in the morning (I had to work that morning anyway), and as long as he could get back to his wife in time for dinner. The timing was perfect.

Justin wasn't into Christmas; he thought it contrived and too commercial. But I thought this might interest him. I told him, "The only present I want from you is to show up." Lee wasn't big on the idea either, but wanted to make it special for me, since Santa and I were going to the trouble. I bought, and wrapped, three presents each (myself and the dog included), labeled them from Santa, and put all but the dog's presents under a ceiling high, forest fresh and aromatic, Frazer Fir, to enjoy while waiting for Christmas to arrive. The dog's presents were a bone, and yummy smelling treats I didn't want him to devour prematurely. I thought I was going to be the only one giving presents, but Lee gave Justin a car seat cover for his dog in case there was any need to take him in my car. Lee also gave me a present, but he gave it to me before Christmas because he wanted to keep it private. It was a compass. He explained that it was so that I could always find my way back to his friendship.

Lee had become a dear friend to me. We did a lot for each other, helped each other, looked out for each other. It was a very mutual relationship of many years that covered a period of terrible demons of alcoholism to great success at sobriety for him. He never failed to remind me that he had succeeded in all he had become because of his close circle of friends, including me, and then he would list off all his close friends. He always included his love for his dad, Danny, and sister, April.

ICOM

In January I got involved with the Interfaith Coalition on Immigration (ICOM), which helps families that are being torn apart because of one or more members having undocumented status. These members are detained, and threatened with deportation. ICOM provides legal assistance and bail for detainees slated for deportation, and helps their families with food, bills, and other necessities. It also holds demonstrations at the Federal Building where ICE operates, and writes letters to get immigrants and undocumented persons out of jail using COVID 19 endangerment as reason enough. I knew the main organizer from church, Daniel Romero. He had been our Minister of Faith Formation, and was now setting off on his own, building ICOM.

Seven members from a related organization in Chicago wanted to come to town to support, and attempt to bail out, one of their members held in detention here in Minneapolis. Daniel was seeking places that would put them up for the night of the hearing. I asked Lee and Justin if we could house two of them.

They said yes. I also told Daniel I would supply some money towards bail, and make a pot of chili for them for dinner. I asked Lee and Justin if we could have the dining room to ourselves, because the group would probably want to talk about the day, and hold a planning meeting. I promised they could share in the chili, and cooked the hamburger separate so that Justin, and any other vegan, could eat it too.

I made a huge pot of chili, bought guacamole, chips, and parmesan cheese to sprinkle on top. I made up the couch into a bed, and put out fresh towels, and new bars of soap. Then, around 1:00 PM, Daniel called and said the folk from Chicago weren't going to stay the night after all. The plea had been unsuccessful; they were discouraged and wanted to drive home right away that night. Now I had mountains of food that I didn't want to go to waste. I called several friends and invited them over, and told Justin and Lee they were welcome to join us. Justin took me up on it, but Lee said, "No, you go be with your friends. Just bring me up some chili with lots of meat in it." He was down, seemed to feel unwanted, unloved, alone and lost. I made him up a BIG bowl of chili with more meat than beans, sprinkled it generously with parmesan cheese. I cut him a thick slice of my rye bread no one else was getting, because I knew he loved rye bread so much, and gave him a huge spoonful of guacamole. When I gave it to him I pleaded, "I wish you would come down. This is a different group than the one I was originally inviting."

He just shook his head. "No, I'll be fine this way." He had already taken his "leg" off.

HOW COULD IT BE?!

It was Friday, February 14, Valentine's Day. I had a doctor's appointment in the morning, came home for lunch, and then was heading straight to Northfield to visit my parents for Valentines weekend. Lee was coming in the door just as I finished eating.

"So, you are going to your parents now?"

"Yup, just about ready." I followed him up the stairs to get my bags.

"Well, Happy Valentine's Day."

"You said that to me yesterday already," I replied.

"Well I am saying it again."

I thought about wishing him the same, but instead just said, "Thank you!"

"Need help with your bags?"

"Naw, I got them. Thanks, though."

Lee looked a little down as he turned to go into his room. And I was on my way, excitedly looking forward to seeing my folks.

When I got to my parents, they came out to greet me, even though it was quite cold. I gave them the flowers, card and blueberries I had brought for them. (Blueberries instead of a box of assorted chocolates, as Mom is pre-diabetic.) We had a very enjoyable evening, and Saturday morning we went to a memorial service for a friend of my parents who had been special to me as well. In the evening, we went to a fundraising dance for the library. We stayed a little while. Dad chatted with some friends while Ma and I tried to follow the dance teacher. But the sound level soon became unbearable for me when the band came out and replaced the canned music. I got up and went to the restroom, covering my ears, and my parents followed me out.

Even though I had planned to stay with my folks until mid Monday, we all decided it would be best if I went home Sunday, because a big snow storm was supposed to hit Monday morning. My Mom had a doctor appointment at the Mayo in Rochester in the afternoon, so my folks decided they would leave early in the morning before the snow came. I did not want to drive in snow either. I got home Sunday afternoon, and thought it awfully quiet from Lee's room, even given that he had been holing up there a lot. Monday passed, and I still had not heard any sound coming from Lee's room. Not so much as his porch door opening and closing so he could have a smoke. I asked my other housemate, Justin, if he knew where Lee was. The answer was no.

When Tuesday came, I became worried. I knocked lightly on the door.

"Lee, are you there?" If he was, he was sound asleep. An hour later, I knocked again, with no answer.

Lee usually called me when he was in the hospital, so I would know what was going on and not worry. I thought about how Lee always used to say, "I would take a bullet for my friends!" How he would "never leave anyone behind." How he searched and searched for Bill, until he finally found him. I realized, that as a proper "Big Sister" to Lee, it was now my turn to start investigating. First, I called the three hospitals where Lee usually ended up. He was not at any of them. Then I called his close friends. Nobody had seen him recently. I remembered his fear that he would be shot while doing EMS. I decided I should go to the Holiday and Taco Bell to see if they knew anything. As I was ready to leave, I noticed Lee's keys and work gloves on the counter. After having been locked out a couple of times, he did start carrying his keys with him most of the time, so I figured it was most likely that he was at home, in his room. I pounded hard on his door, to wake him if he were sleeping.

"Lee, if you don't want to talk to me, just tell me to go away, and I will!" Still no answer. Afraid I might catch him nude in bed, and thinking it really was not my place to go looking in his room as I was the "landlady" and only supposed to enter a renter's room to make repairs, I tentatively opened the door.

I was not ready for what I saw. Lee was curled up on the floor, his face purple except for his forehead. He was squeezed between two chairs one of which had toppled on it's side, the wood one that apparently had had his computer on the seat. I was unsure whether it was the chair or the computer that had bruised his face. He was not wearing his prosthetic, and he faced his bed, as if he had fallen off of the bed while reaching over. I immediately called 911.

"Is he alive; is he breathing?"

I put my hand on his side that was up. "Yes! It is very faint, but he is breathing! And then I counted out, "Now, now, now, now, now…" to give an idea of how fast he was breathing. He was also trying to open his eye, would get it about half way open, then let close again.

"We'll get some paramedics over right away. Stay with him. What is the address?"

I told her the address, trying not to sound too panicky. Then I called out to Justin, please go unlock the doors, and let the paramedics in!!!"

He did go downstairs, but didn't seem to get the urgency, so when the paramedics arrived (and they were very fast), I started to rush downstairs to bring them up to Lee's room. But when I took my hand off Lee's side, he exhaled big.

I left in a panic, "He is this way!" I told the paramedics. There were three of them.

They looked at him and pronounced him dead.

"Please, try to revive him!"

"No, he has been dead a long time; his body is cold."

"We keep our house very cold; of course he'd be cold from being so still!"

I touched his leg. It was very cold. But then, he was only wearing shorts and a lightweight shirt, and we keep the house at 67*F, and this is the coldest room in the house.

"No, the blood is pooling on the underside of his body. He has been dead a long time," the paramedic continued.

They did not look under his shirt to verify that, merely touched his neck, which was pale. If they were referring to the bruise on his face, it was also on the upper side as well as the front.

"When did you last see him?," another paramedic asked.

"Friday, just after lunch."

"He's been dead for days."

"But I just saw him breathing, and his eye lid move!"

"I am sorry, but it was just your imagination; he has been dead for days."

I stopped fighting. I know what I saw. But then, Lee had said that if he had a heart attack or something, he did not want to be brought back to life. That is when they turned to the dirty green cloth on the floor, with four or five needles and a spoon on it.

"Did he take drugs?"

"He was an EMS, They might be from that."

"It looks like he was using Heroin."

I was dumbfounded. Lee? Who was always treating drug addicts? Who looked down on drug addicts? Who helped me get rid of an addict from renting with me? But there it was.

"It looks like he stuck a needle between his toes."

Lee had told me that drug addicts would shoot it up between the toes so as not to be discovered. Unbelievably, I was not mad at Lee. Had I found out he was using while he was alive, I don't know what I would have done. Probably kicked him out. But now, I was just sorrowful, and wanted him back.

"We've done all we can here, and have already called the police to come out and do their investigation. Could you do something with the dog so he doesn't get in the way of the police?"

I asked Justin to please take his dog into his room and go be with him so he didn't feel imprisoned. The police asked me to leave Lee's room while they looked around. I took this opportunity to call Lee's Dad, Danny, in Connecticut, and then his mentor, Denny. The coroner arrived shortly thereafter. After she talked to the police, she did her own review of the situation. When she came downstairs, I asked, "What about trying Narcan?"

She looked sadly at me, and replied, "I found his box of Narcan. It was empty. There is nothing you could have done."

She took photos of the phone numbers and addresses of Danny, and of Denny when I told her that Denny and Jane had been like parents to Lee. By now, it was 9:30 PM, and the coroner said she would do the autopsy in the morning, and wanted Lee's dad to call her. She let me know that since I was not a relative, they would not tell me the results of the autopsy, but I could get it from Lee's dad if he cared to share the information. However, the next day, she would not give the information to Lee's dad either, since he was "only" a step-dad. She wanted a blood relative, even though Lee and Danny had been tight.

And so, I got a call from Lee's younger brother, Mark, the one who ran Worm Town, the one with whom Lee was having a hard time meeting to talk to about care for their dad and sister.

"When would you like me to come pick up Lee's things—I'll be out your way Thursday and Friday."

"I've got to work, and it would be nice to have something of a service for Lee with his friends here, too, as well as one in Connecticut."

We decided on Saturday for the service. Mark would contact Lee's Pastor (also Mark), to arrange the details. Denny suggested cremating Lee, and floating his ashes down the Mississippi in a miniature boat. As I was looking over my files to prepare something to say at the service, I discovered notes stating that, indeed, Lee had wanted to be cremated and have his ashes scattered on the Mississippi, and some saved to be sent back to his family or scattered on the Atlantic Ocean. Lee's brother, Mark, agreed to this plan. We would hold the service at the Faith Mennonite Church, great thanks to them for letting us use their building, and then walk to the Franklin Bridge over the Mississippi to scatter a portion of Lee's ashes. I ordered red rose petals from Bachman's, to be picked up Saturday morning fresh, to be scattered over the river with Lee's ashes, and Mark again said this was O.K., maybe because I had already paid for them, or maybe he did think this was a nice gesture.

Mark's wife, Debbie, and daughter, Darra, also flew out. They all came to my house with a rented van Friday night; they wanted to leave Saturday right after the service. I was sure they would need a u-haul because Lee had so much stuff, especially large tools, like a circular saw and table, a compressor, flood lights, a vice, and boxes of tools. But the three of them were expert packers. Clothing they took to the Good Will, or trashed. Everything of value they were able to get in the van. It was magic, but then, packing vans with merchandise is what they did for a living. They were extremely efficient too, and respectful of my needs. Once everything was packed, Debbie gave me a big hug, saying, "Take care of yourself, now. See you tomorrow." It was a wonderful, warm hug that I was grateful for and returned in kind. Then I turned to Darra with my arms out, and we hugged each other tightly.

"That's pretty good!," exclaimed Debbie. "Darra is not a hugger, not even for me. All I get is this…" and Darra and Debbie tilted their heads together so they just touched.

Then I approached Mark for a hug. He had been all business earlier, but now he let his emotions show, doing his best to be strong and hold back tears. "Yes, see you tomorrow."

Saturday morning I went to pick up the rose petals. They were everything I could want. Big, ruby red with a spot of yellow on the inner corner, fresh and moist. Bachman's didn't have a basket like I imagined, but directed me to a store a couple of blocks away , Michael's, where I might get one. Perfect.

The service was simple, but nice. Pastor Mark had made up sheets of the order of service. He had found a very becoming picture of Lee, with his winning smile, and a snorkel mask in his hands. First there was a welcome and opening prayer, followed by a scripture reading of Psalm 46. Then came the Eulogy, followed by a reading of the poem "Do Not Go Gentle into That Good Night," which had been a favorite of Lee's. After that came memories from friends and family. I spoke first. Several other people spoke, including Lee's brother, and the son of the Pastor, who must have been all of twelve years old. The latter said, "Yea, I guess I have known Lee since, and he paused, since I was born really. He always used to give me nice things, like a drone. I am just a kid, but he used to ask me, '"Do you have a girlfriend yet?"' I'd say, '"No,"' and he would give me some skittles. And that is how it would go every time I saw him. He'd ask, '"Do you have a girlfriend yet?"' and then he would give me some skittles." Another person noted, "He always seemed to come visiting around dinner time."

We walked to the bridge in quiet conversation, making our way around the snow banks and puddles. Pastor Mark gave a closing prayer: "Now, whether it takes a thousand years or only a few, our friend Lee will finally finish the journey down the Mississippi he so longed to complete." Lee's brother, Mark, started to pour the ashes over the wide cement rail, but the wind blew them back in our faces. "It is Lee, coming back to us!," someone said, and there was a little laugher. I watched Mark poured the rest of the ashes though the cement pillars, near the bridge floor. However alive Lee had been when I last saw him there on the floor of his room, he most certainly was dead now. And then I offered the rose petals around to throw through the pillars after the ashes. Folks were only taking a few petals, wanting to be polite.

"Take more! Take a whole handful!" I encouraged. "We have plenty! Send Lee off with Love!"

The bridge was strewn with ash and rose petals. People talked quietly with each other. I threw the last of the rose petals and leaned my head against the cement rail, watching them proceed down the river. It was impossible to see the ash on the water, but the rose petals floated up and down as small dots of color against the black, icy water.

"Good-by, Lee," I said softly. "Good-by. I really DID love you. You were much more than just a brother to me."

AFTERWORD

To do him homage, I retired Lee's bedroom key. I had it made special for him; it had dolphins on it. If Lee had held on just a little bit longer, not given up on HOPE, he might today be again very happy. When Jason, the head of the woodworking shop at Mission Lodge came around to give his condolences, he mentioned that he was leaving Mission Lodge, and had Lee been alive, Jason would have recommended Lee to fill his place. Lee had always coveted Jason's job. And his fishing buddy, Freddie, who had cut him off, had totally lost his anger, had forgotten what the argument was about, and was looking forward to the fishing opener and another season of fishing with Lee.